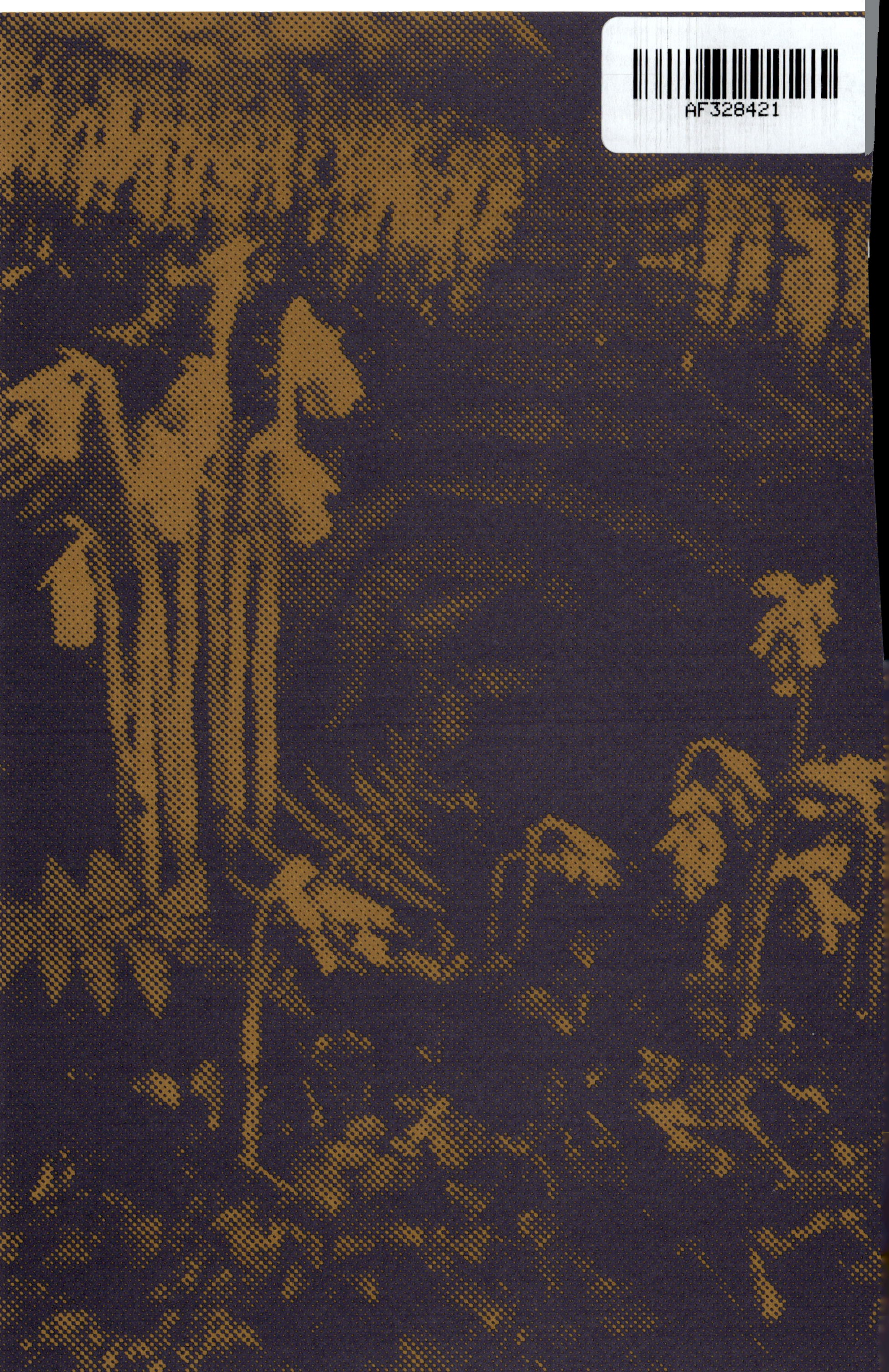

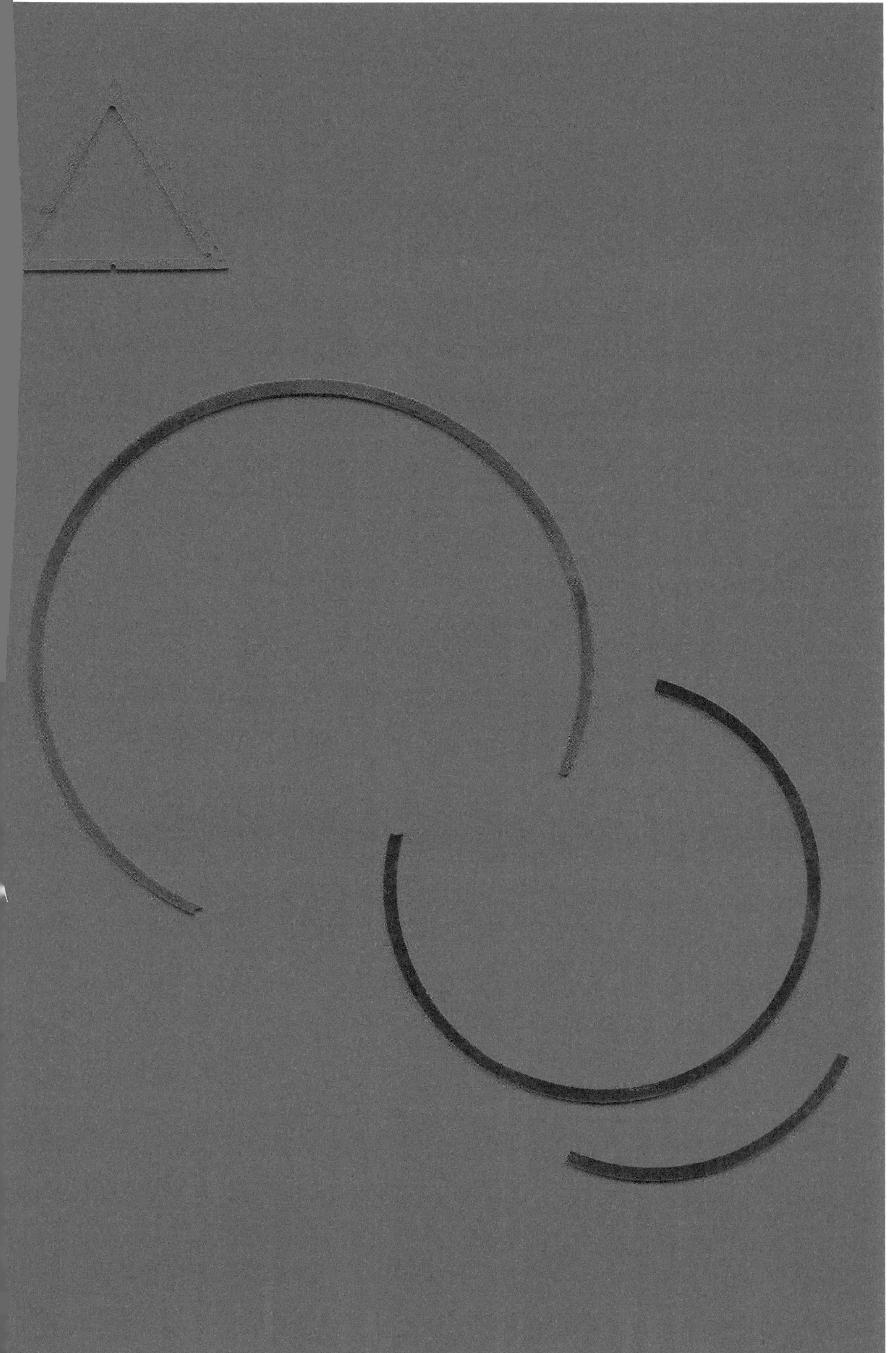

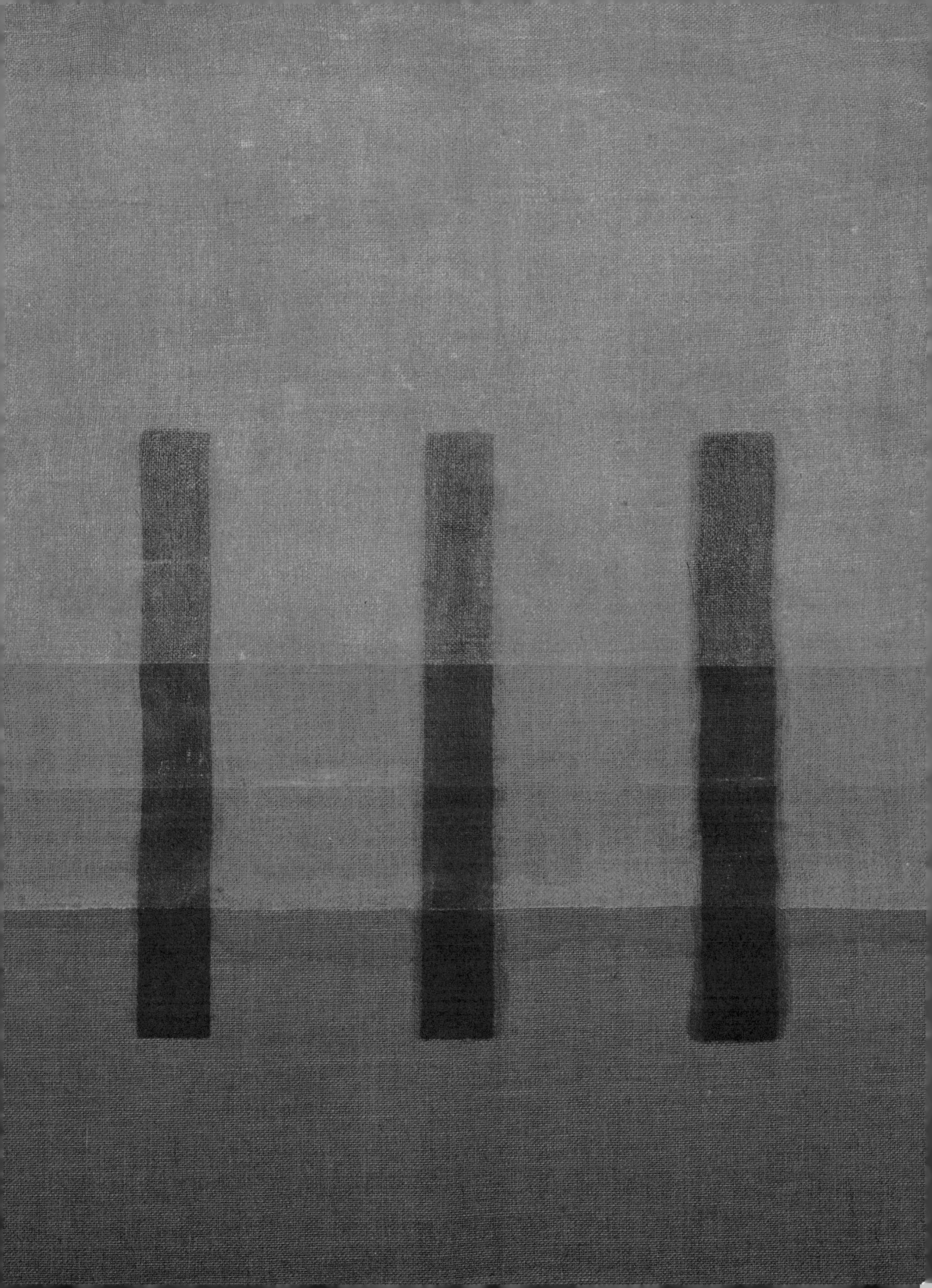

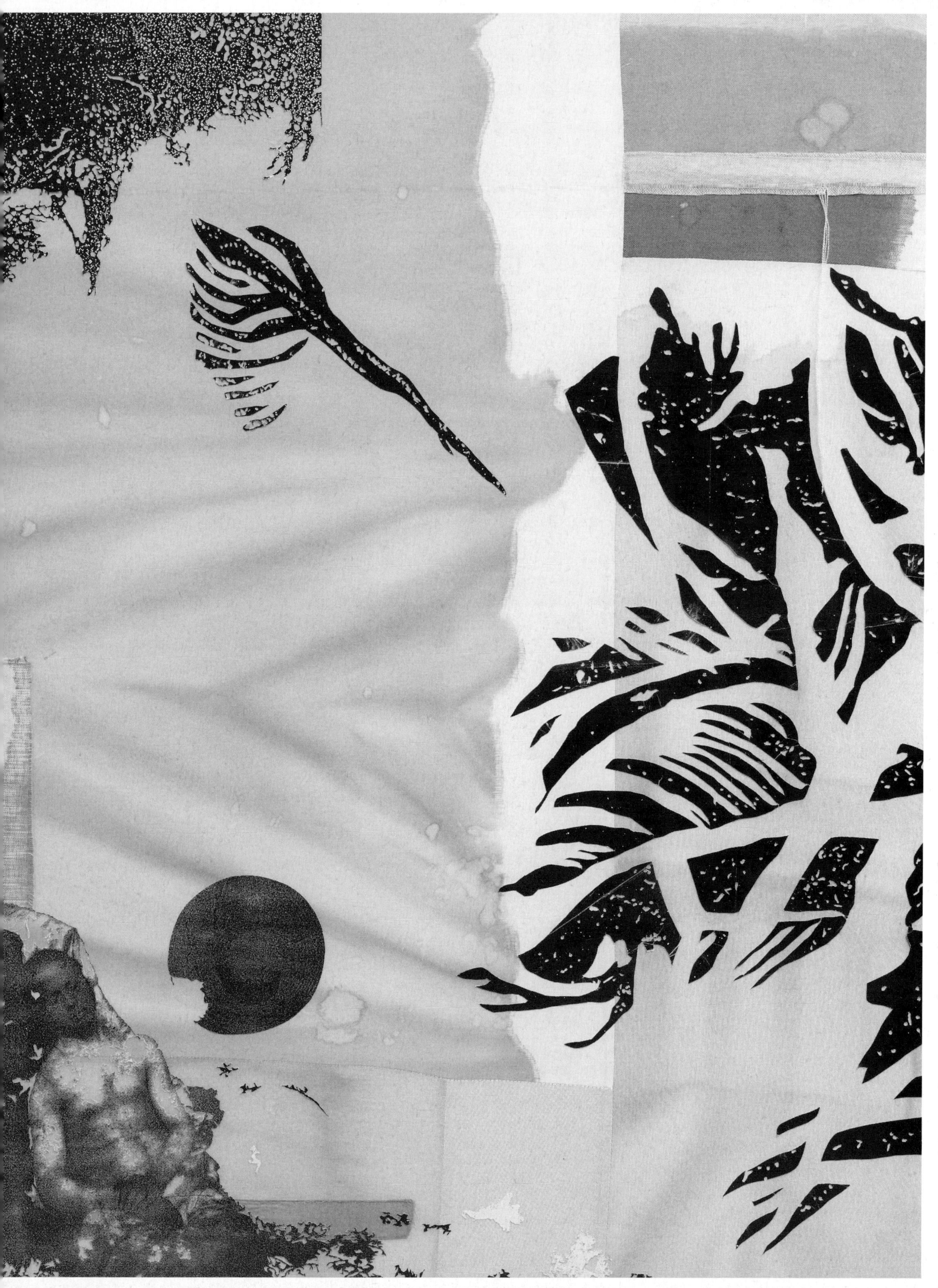

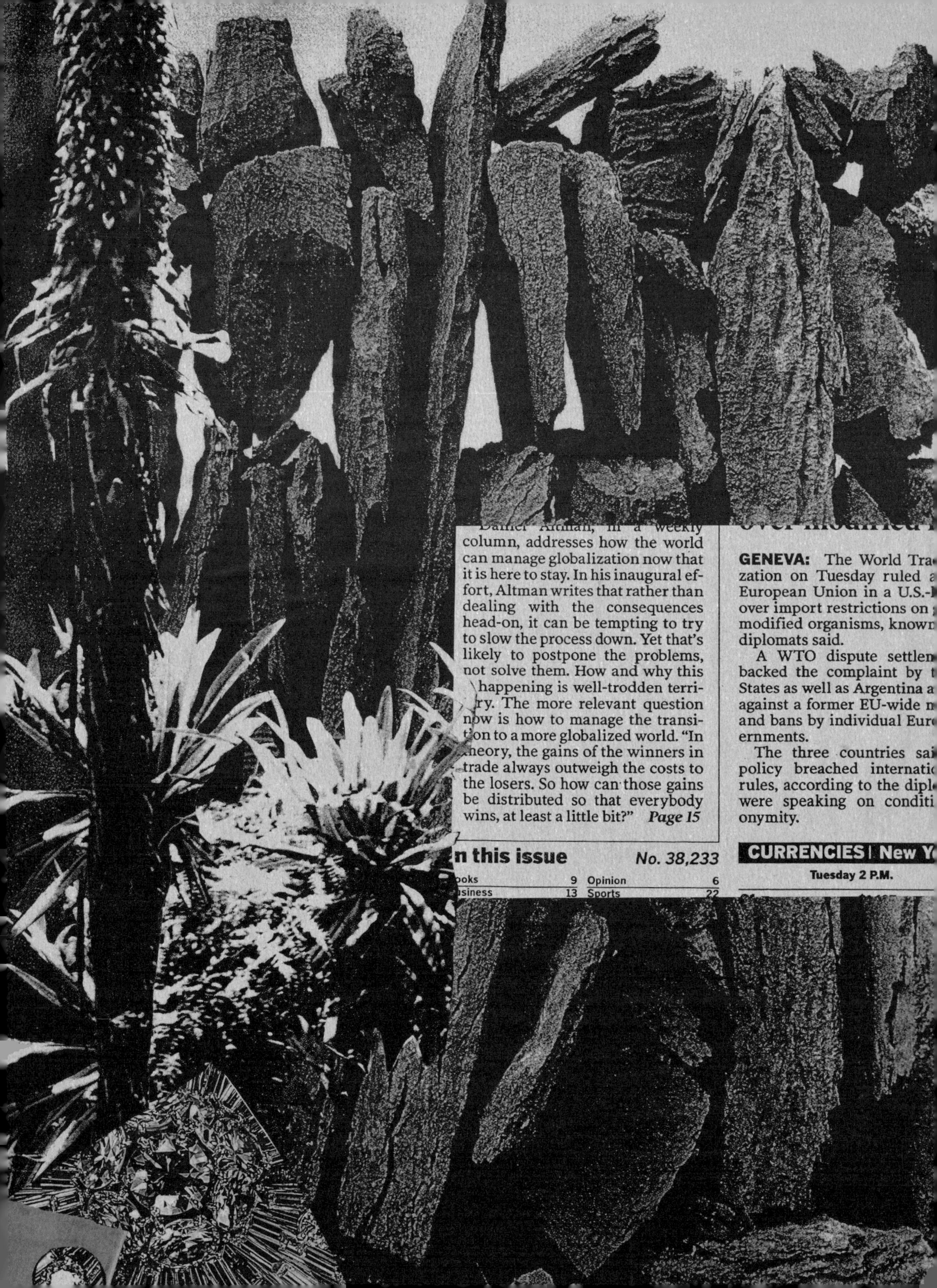

Daniel Altman, in a weekly column, addresses how the world can manage globalization now that it is here to stay. In his inaugural effort, Altman writes that rather than dealing with the consequences head-on, it can be tempting to try to slow the process down. Yet that's likely to postpone the problems, not solve them. How and why this happening is well-trodden territory. The more relevant question now is how to manage the transition to a more globalized world. "In theory, the gains of the winners in trade always outweigh the costs to the losers. So how can those gains be distributed so that everybody wins, at least a little bit?" *Page 15*

GENEVA: The World Tra zation on Tuesday ruled a European Union in a U.S.- over import restrictions on modified organisms, known diplomats said.

A WTO dispute settlen backed the complaint by t States as well as Argentina a against a former EU-wide n and bans by individual Eur ernments.

The three countries sa policy breached internatio rules, according to the dipl were speaking on conditi onymity.

n this issue   No. 38,233

oks	9	Opinion	6
siness	13	Sports	22

CURRENCIES | New Y

Tuesday 2 P.M.

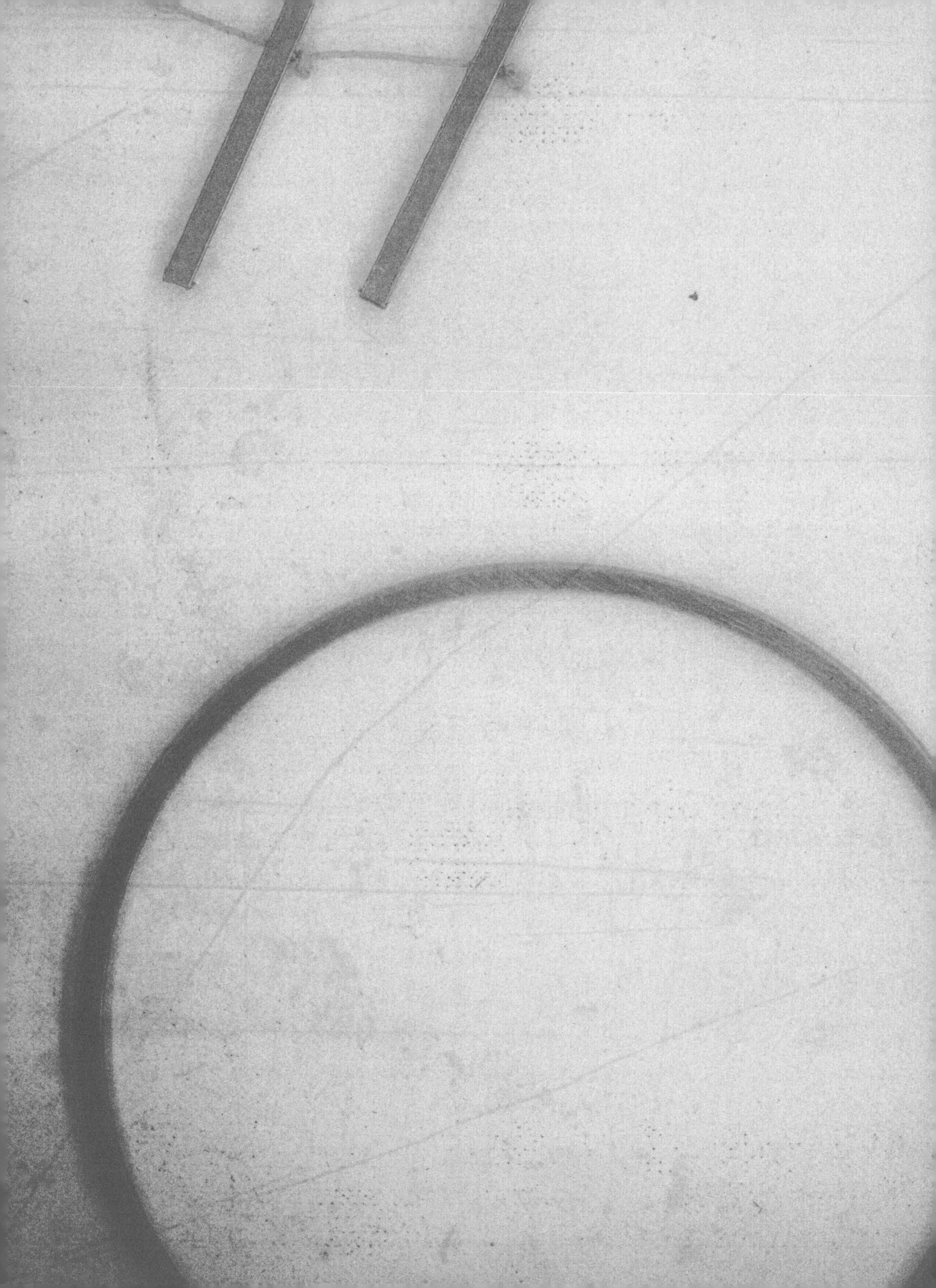

Below Is Turbulence, above Is Direction

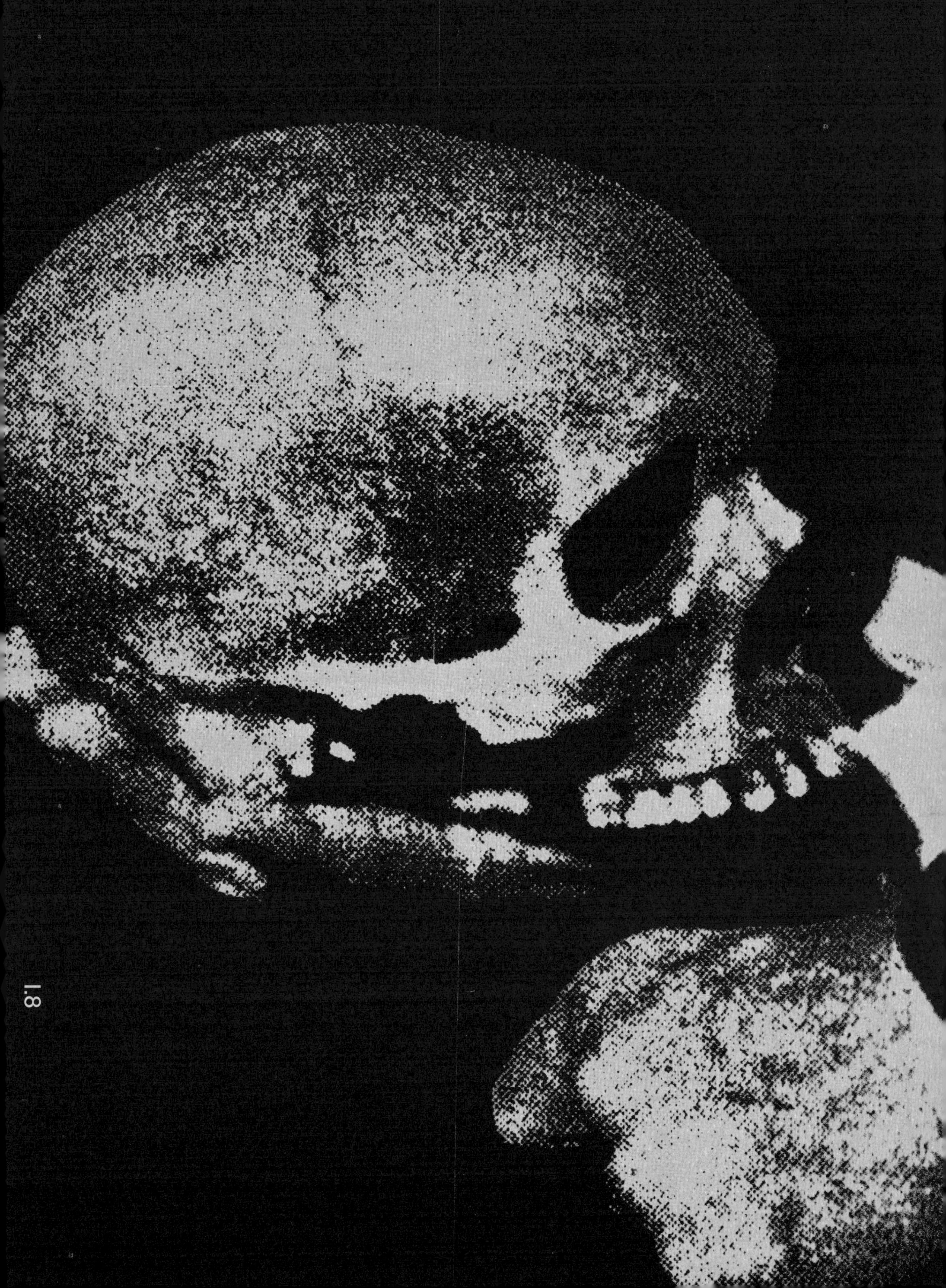

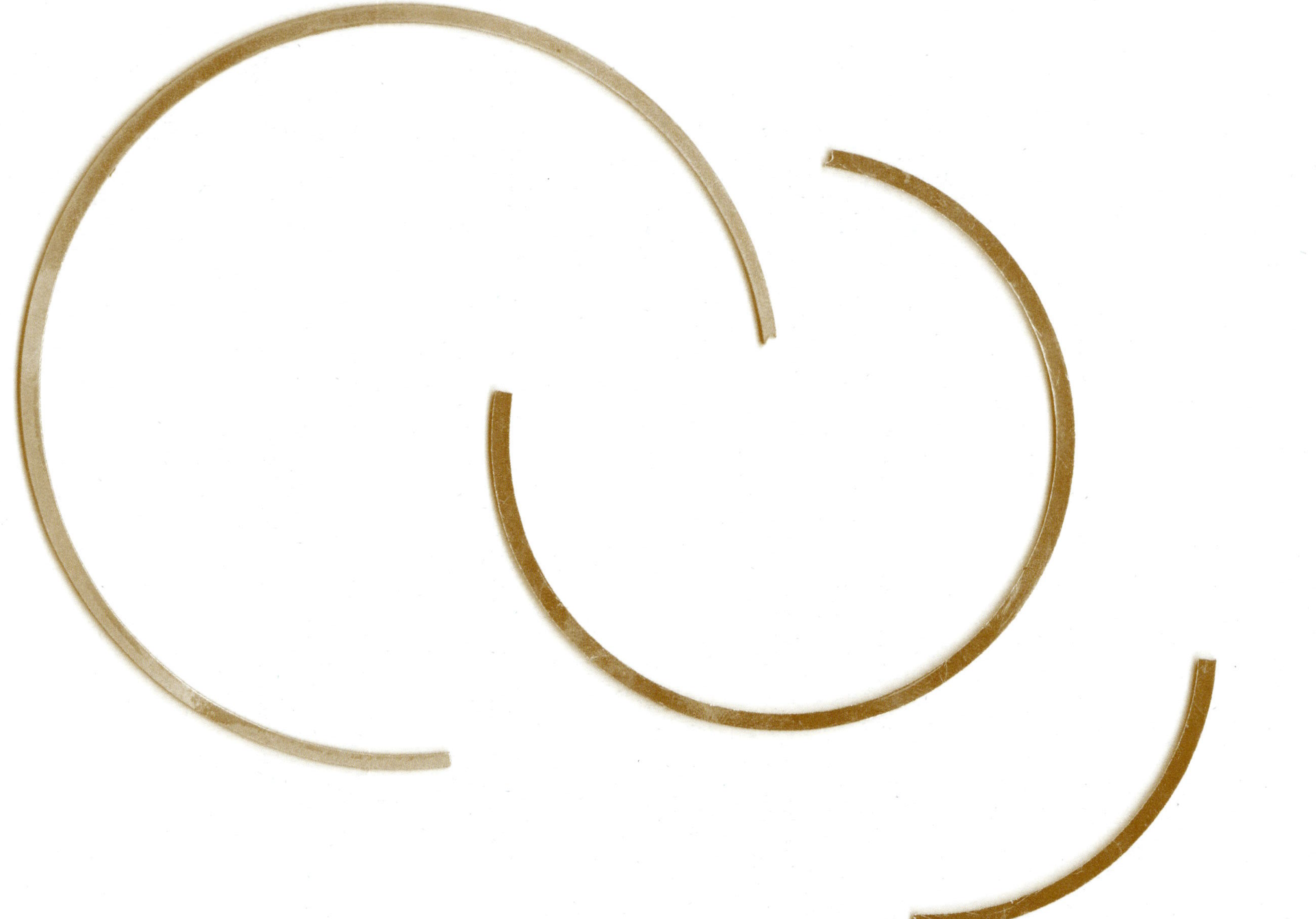

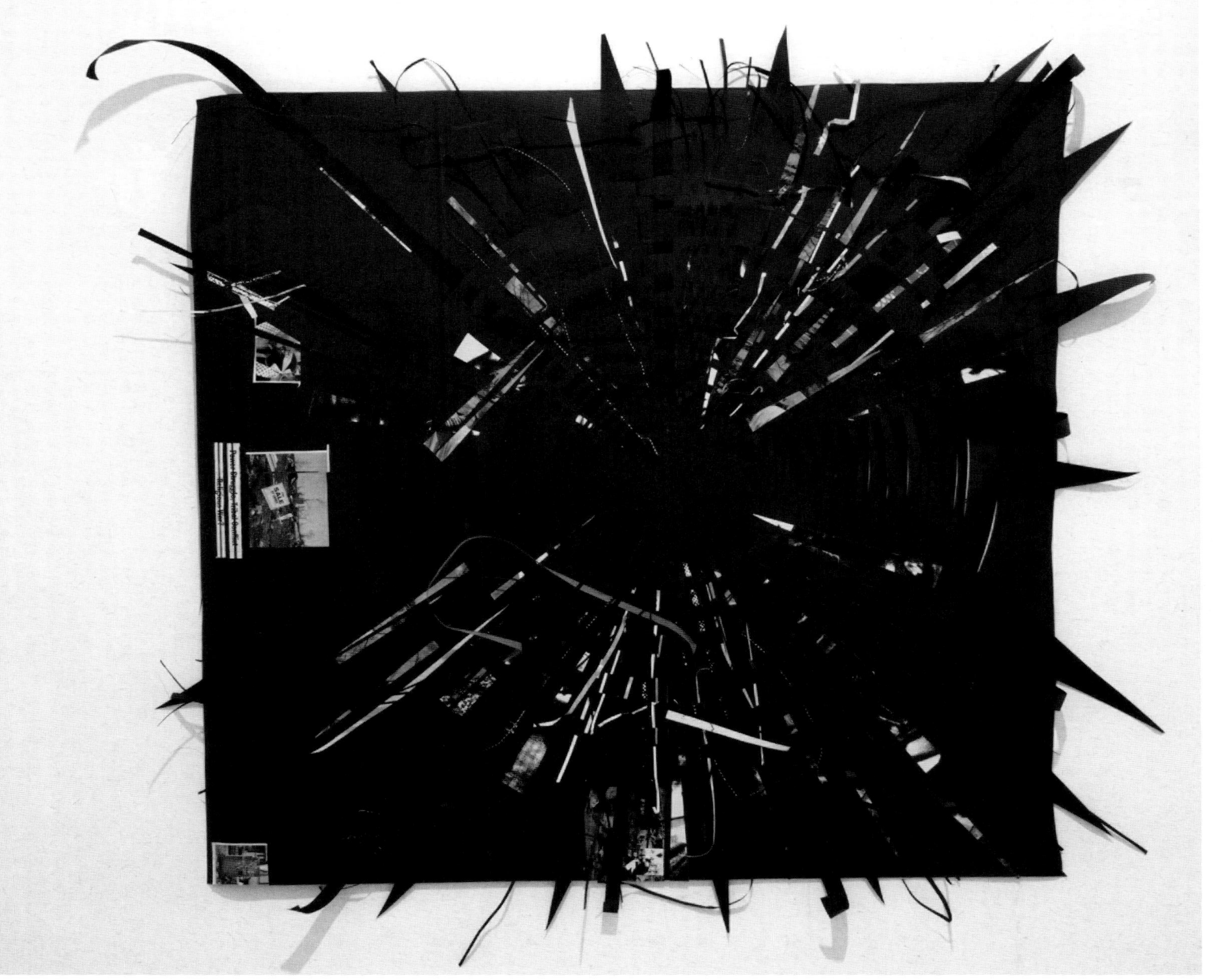

II.3

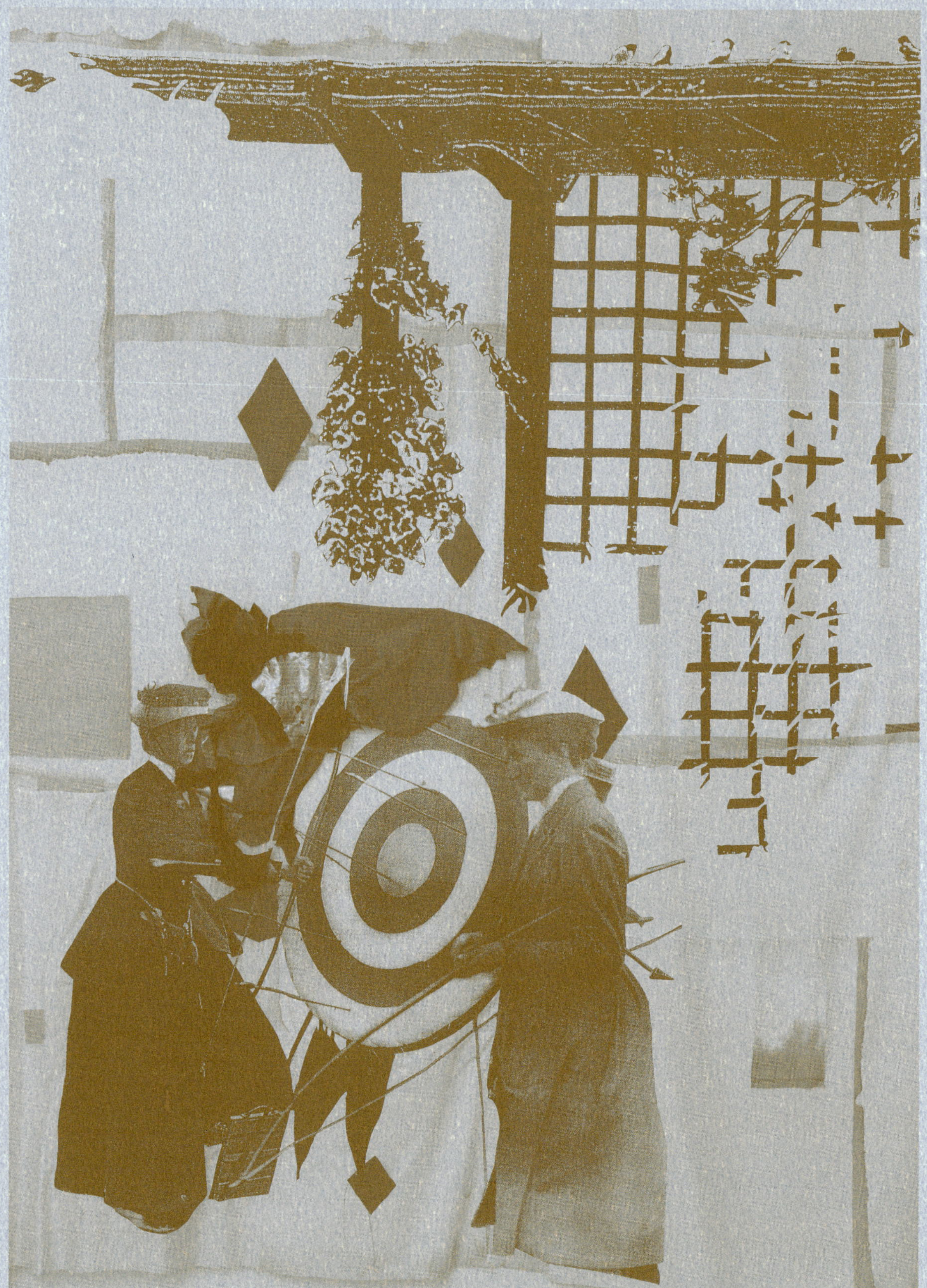

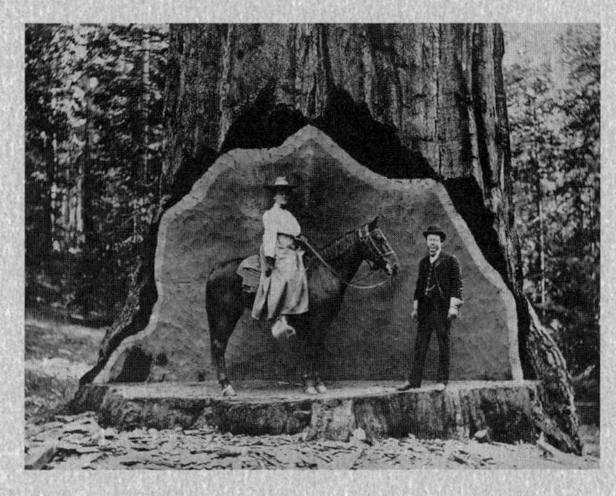

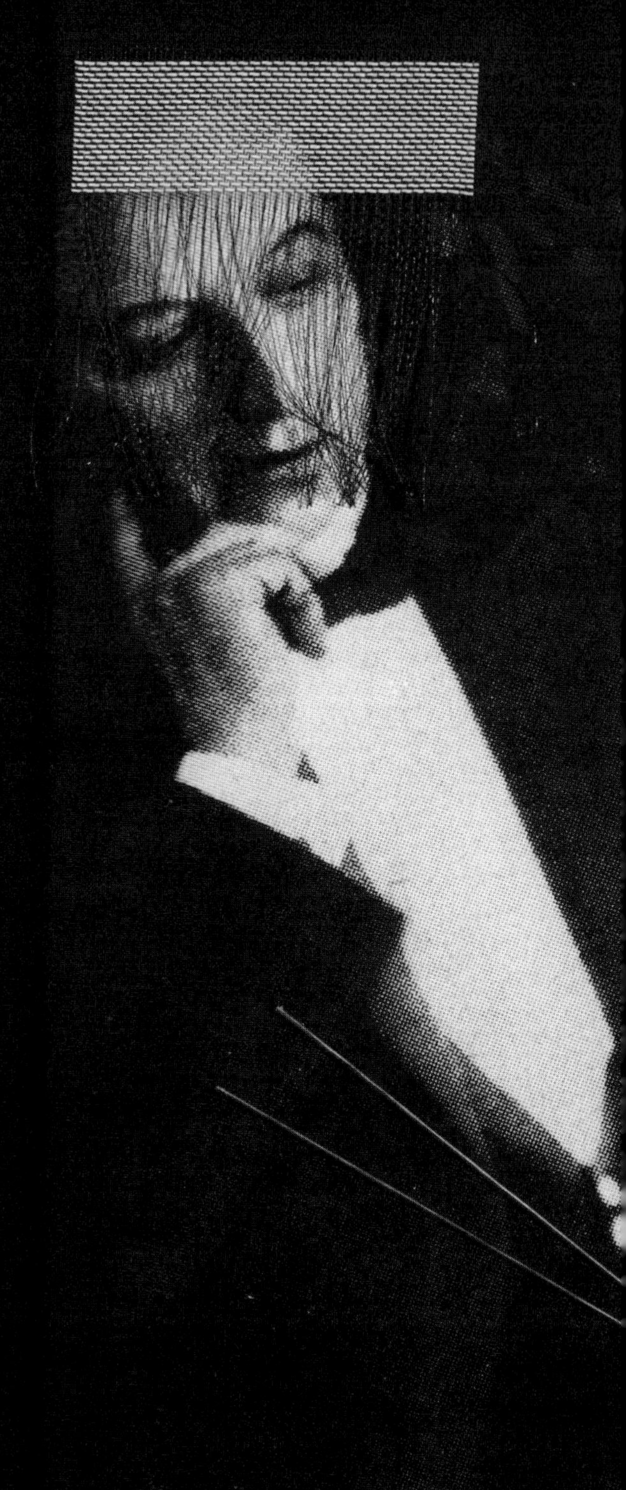

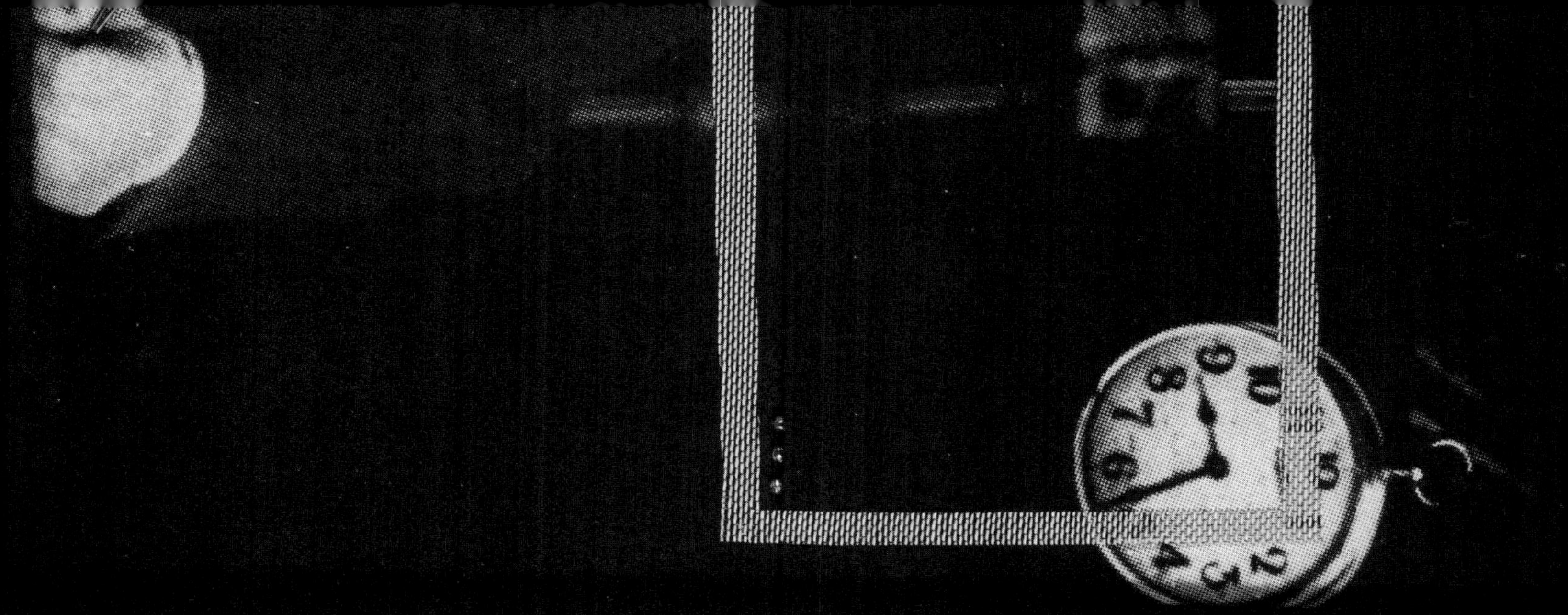

Below Is Fatigue, above Is Sight

II.7

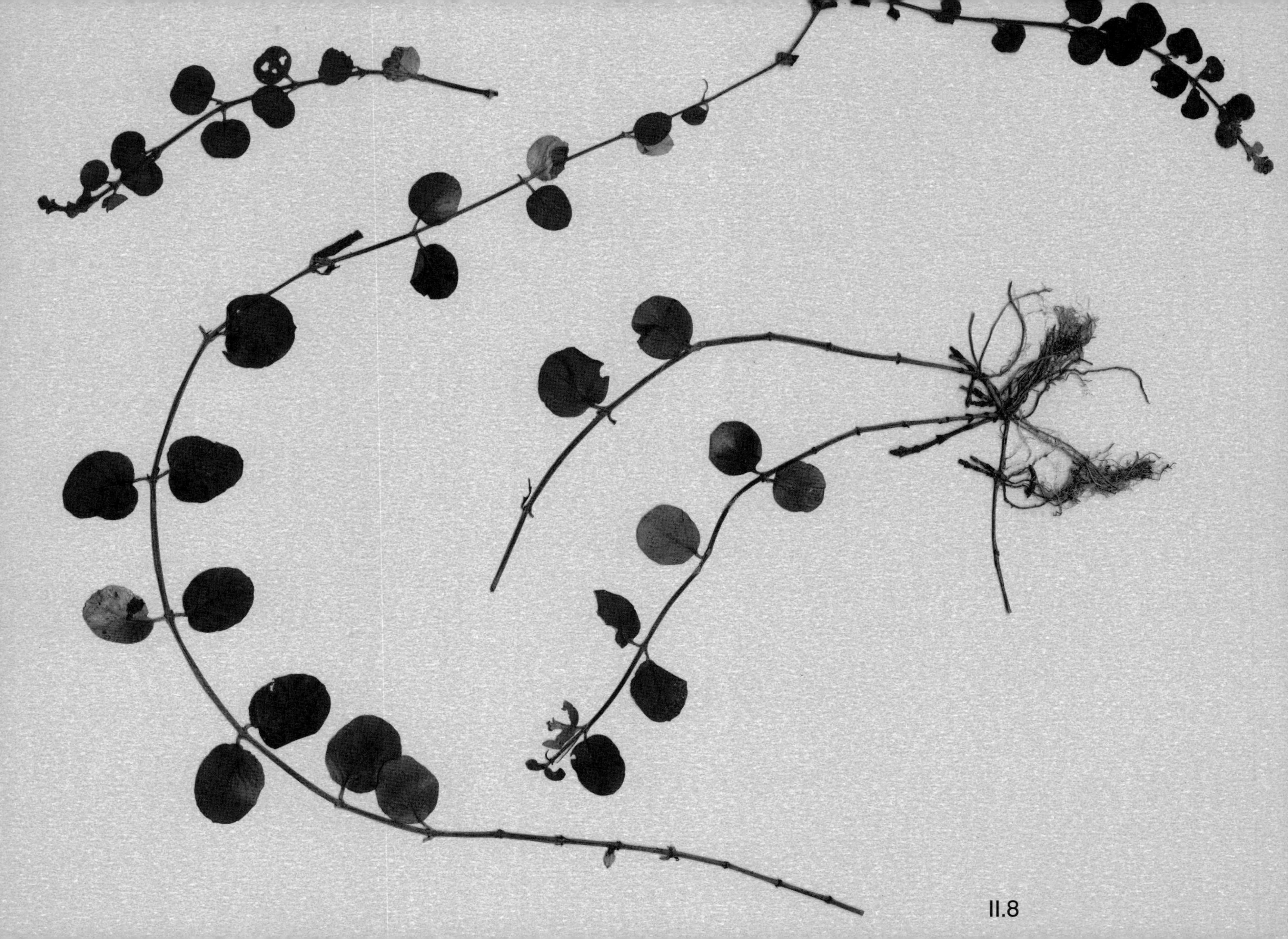

11.8

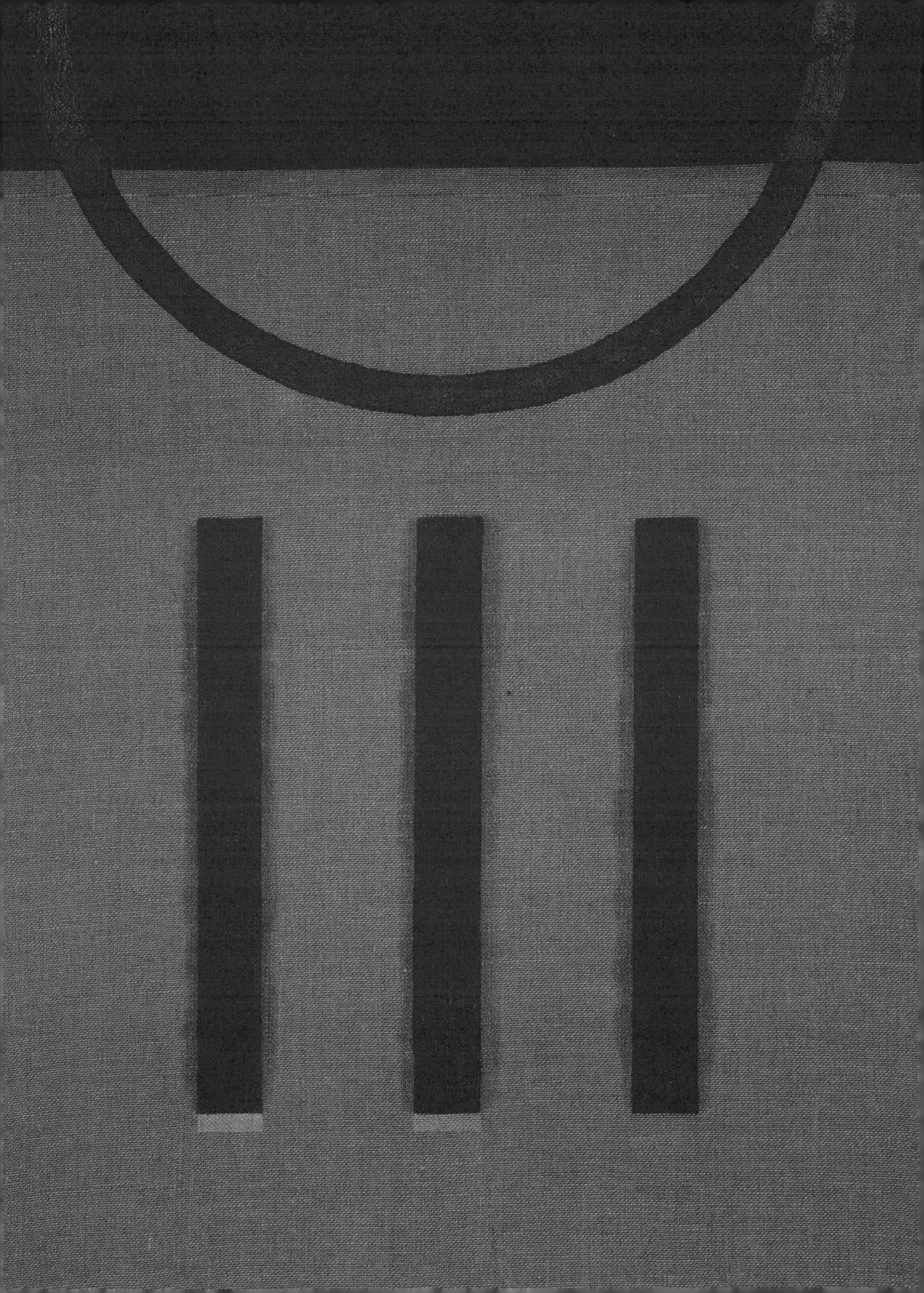

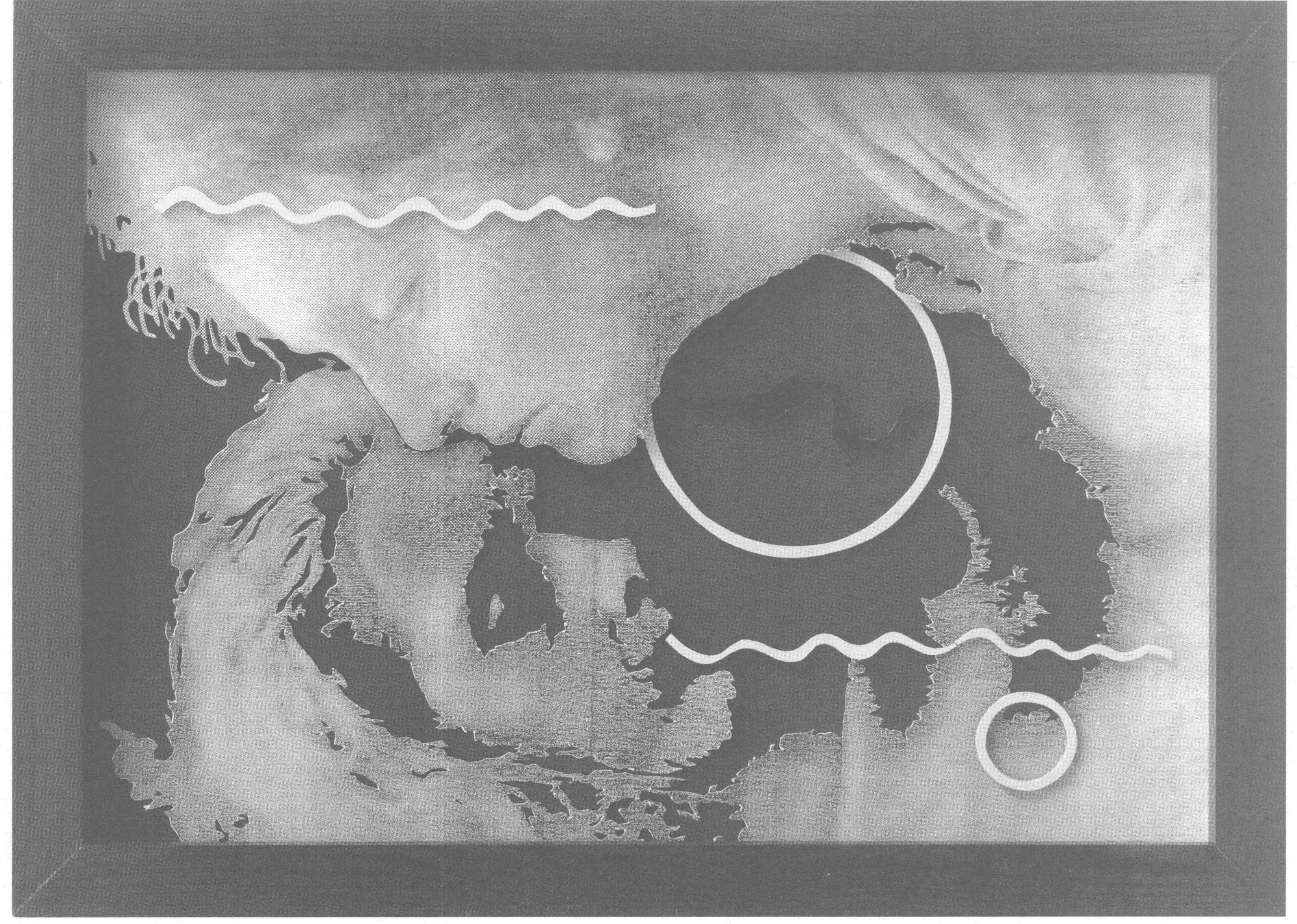

Below Is Sight, above Is Heat

III.2

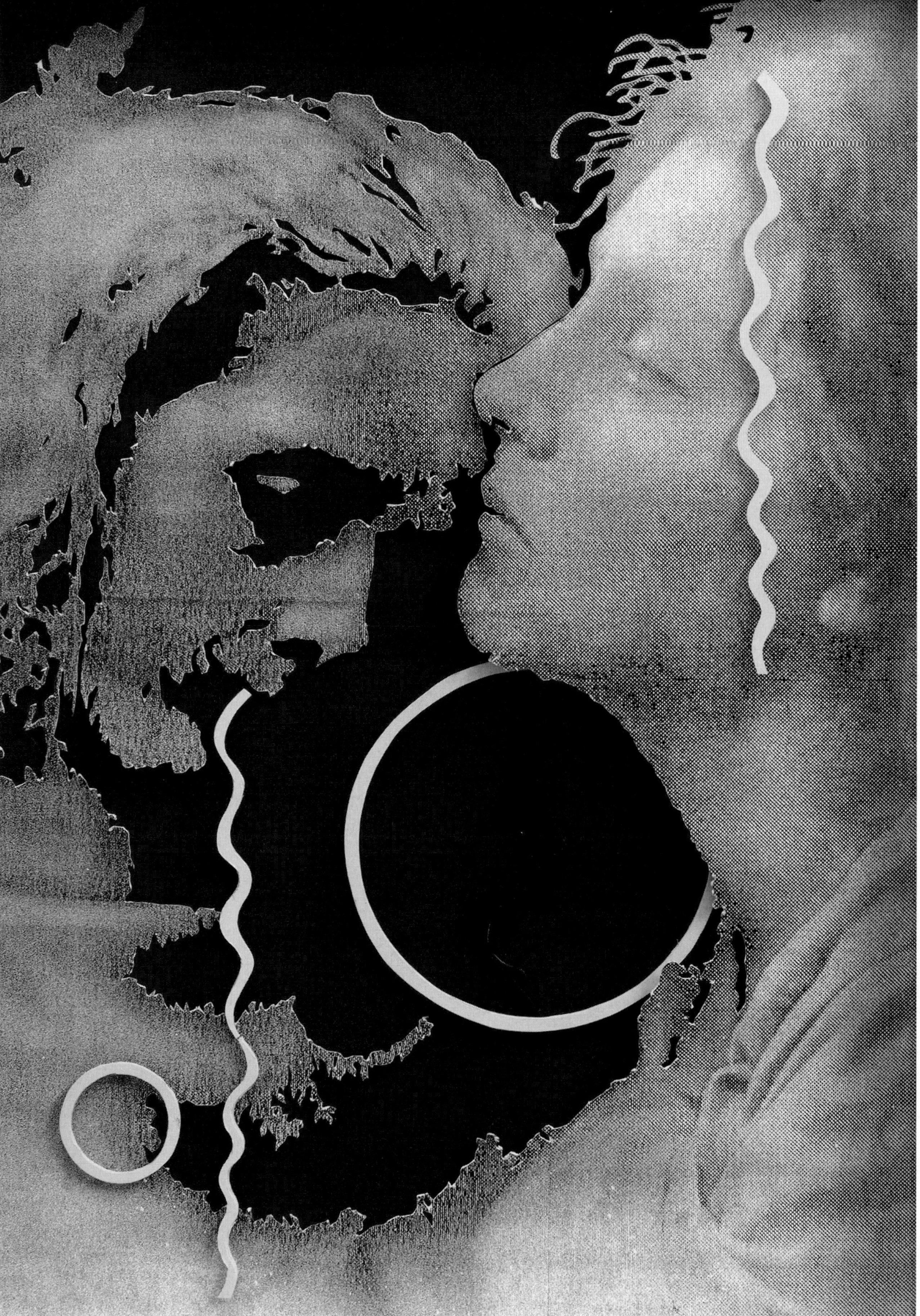

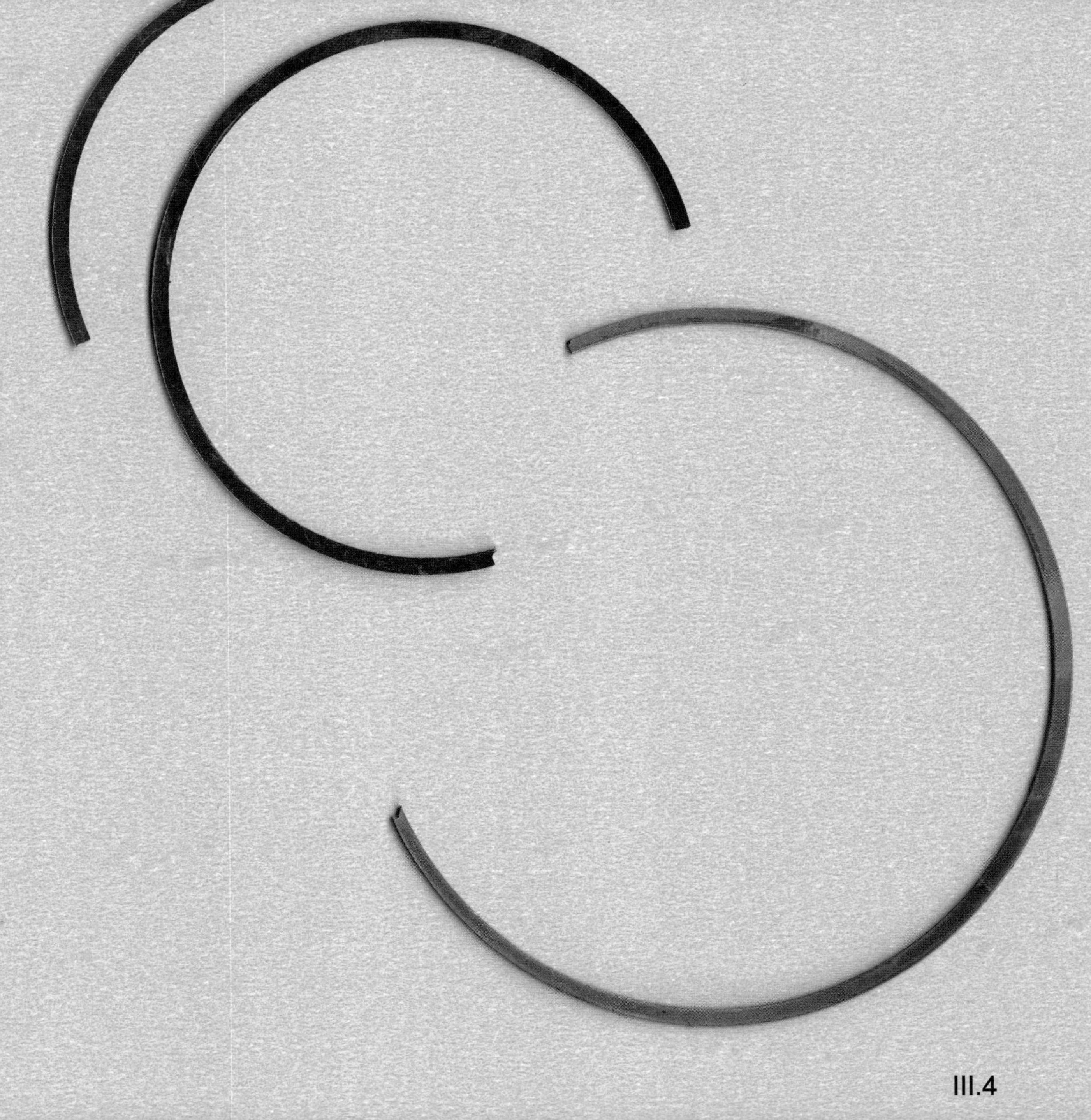

III.4

III.5

TOUCHING

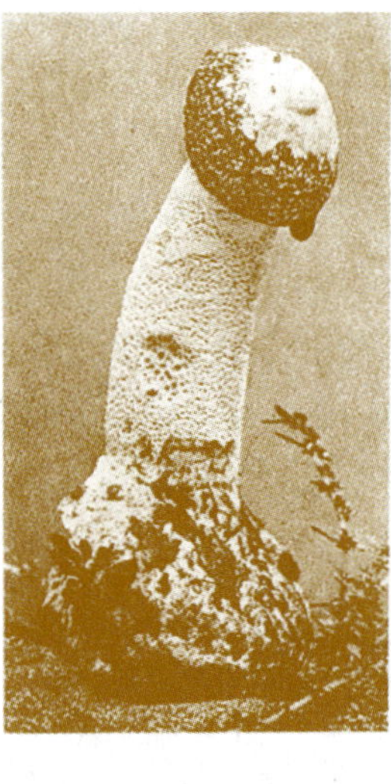

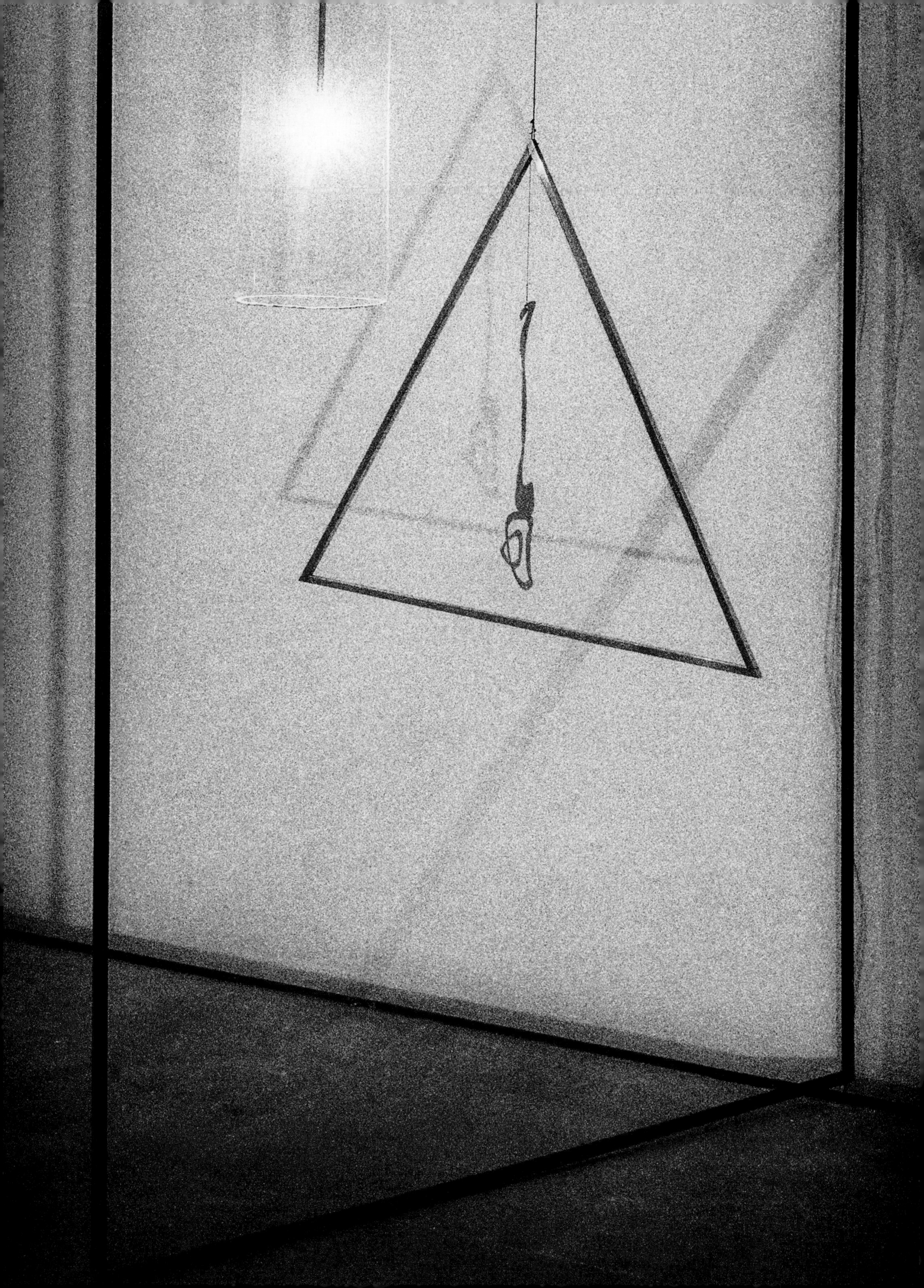

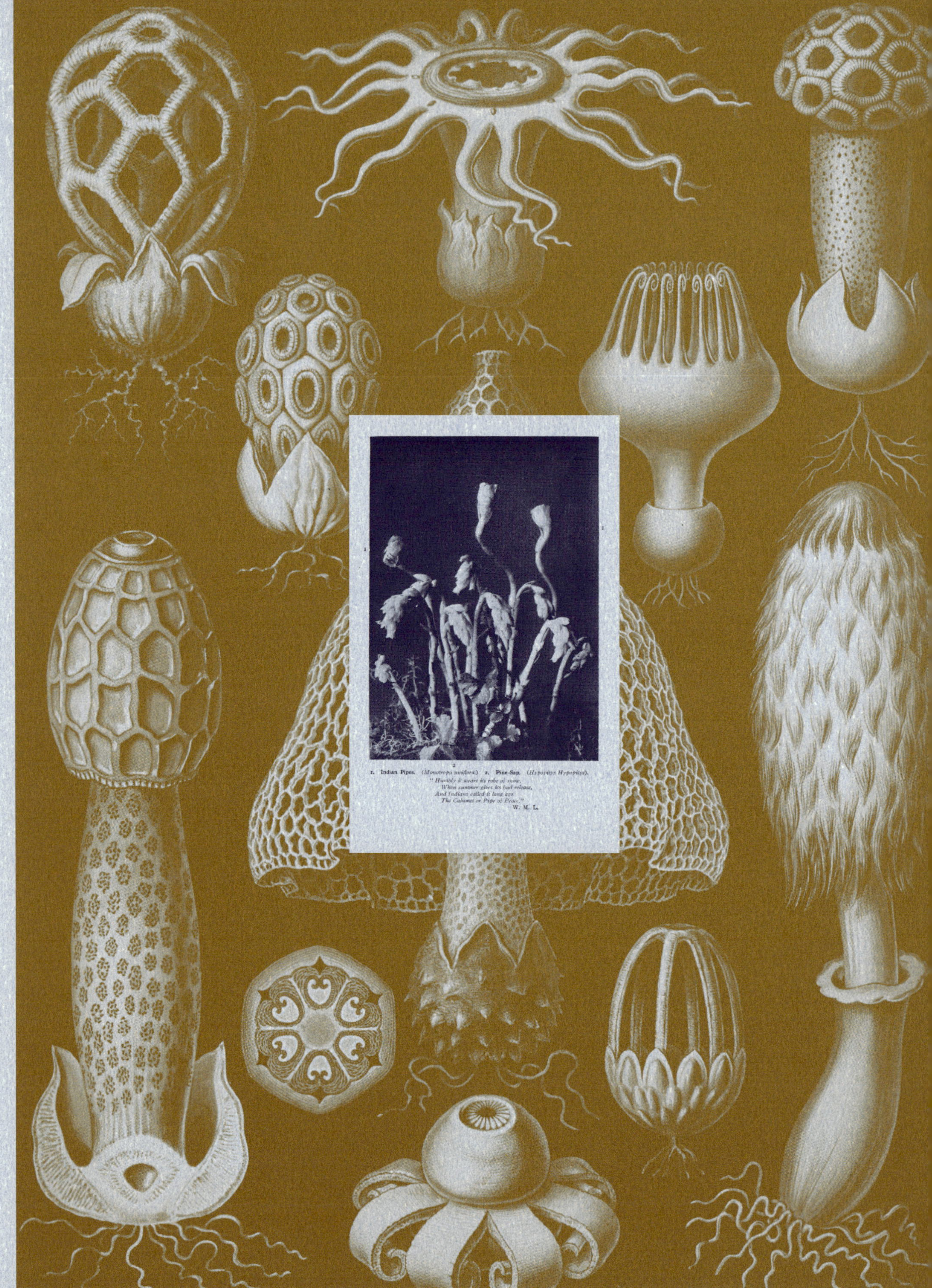

1. Indian Pipes. (*Monotropa uniflora.*)   2. Pine-Sap. (*Hypopitys Hypopitys*).

"Humbly it wears its robe of snow,
   When summer gives its bud release,
   And Indians called it long ago
      The Calumet or Pipe of Peace."

W. M. L.

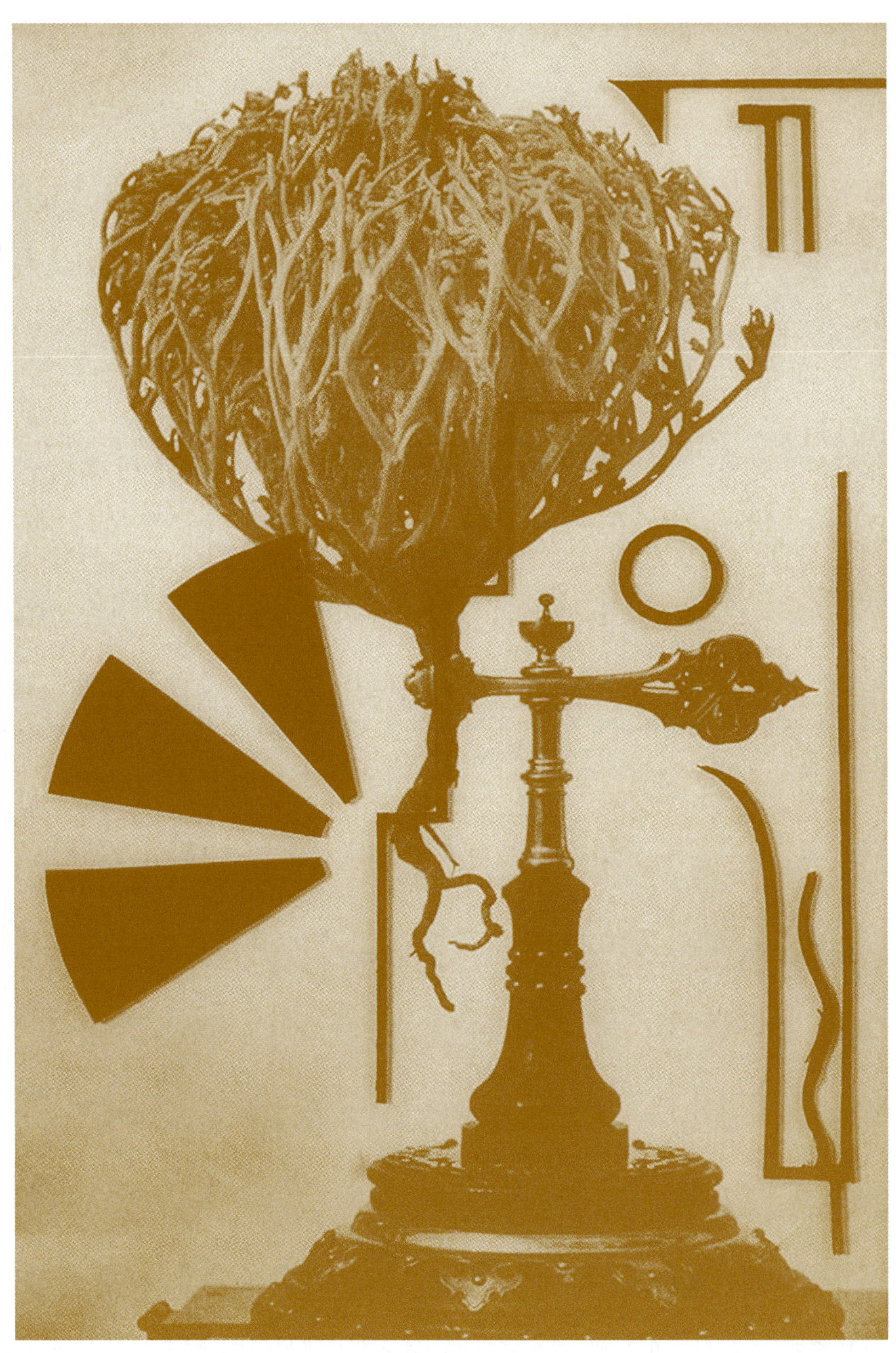

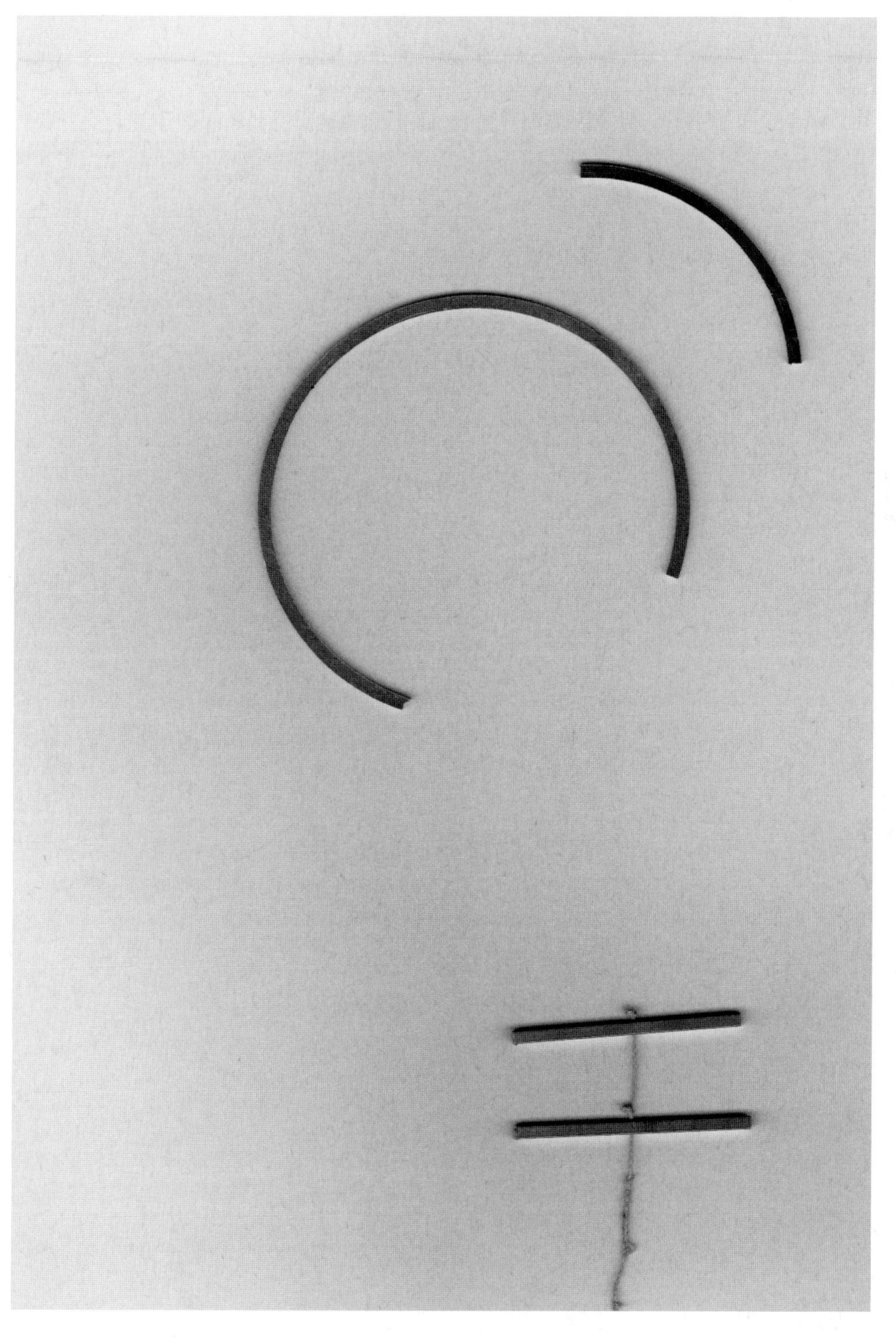

Below Is Stillness, above Is Air

MERGING

IV.4

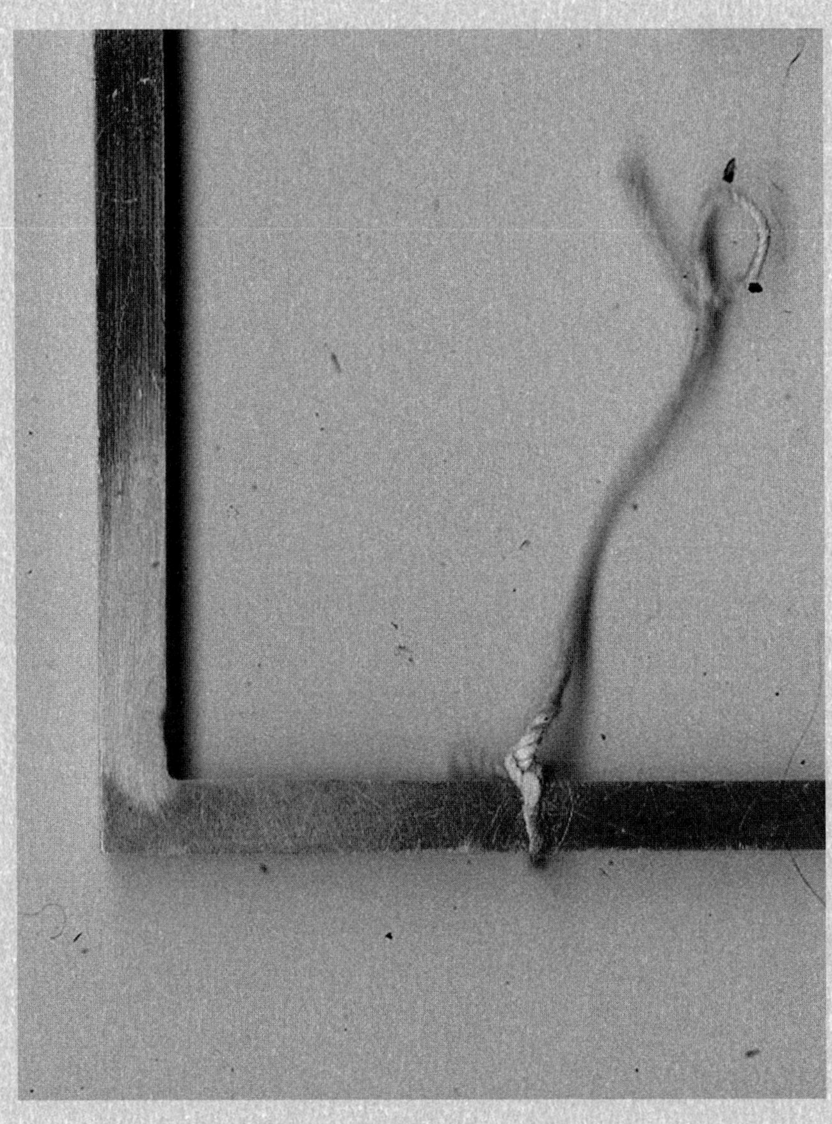

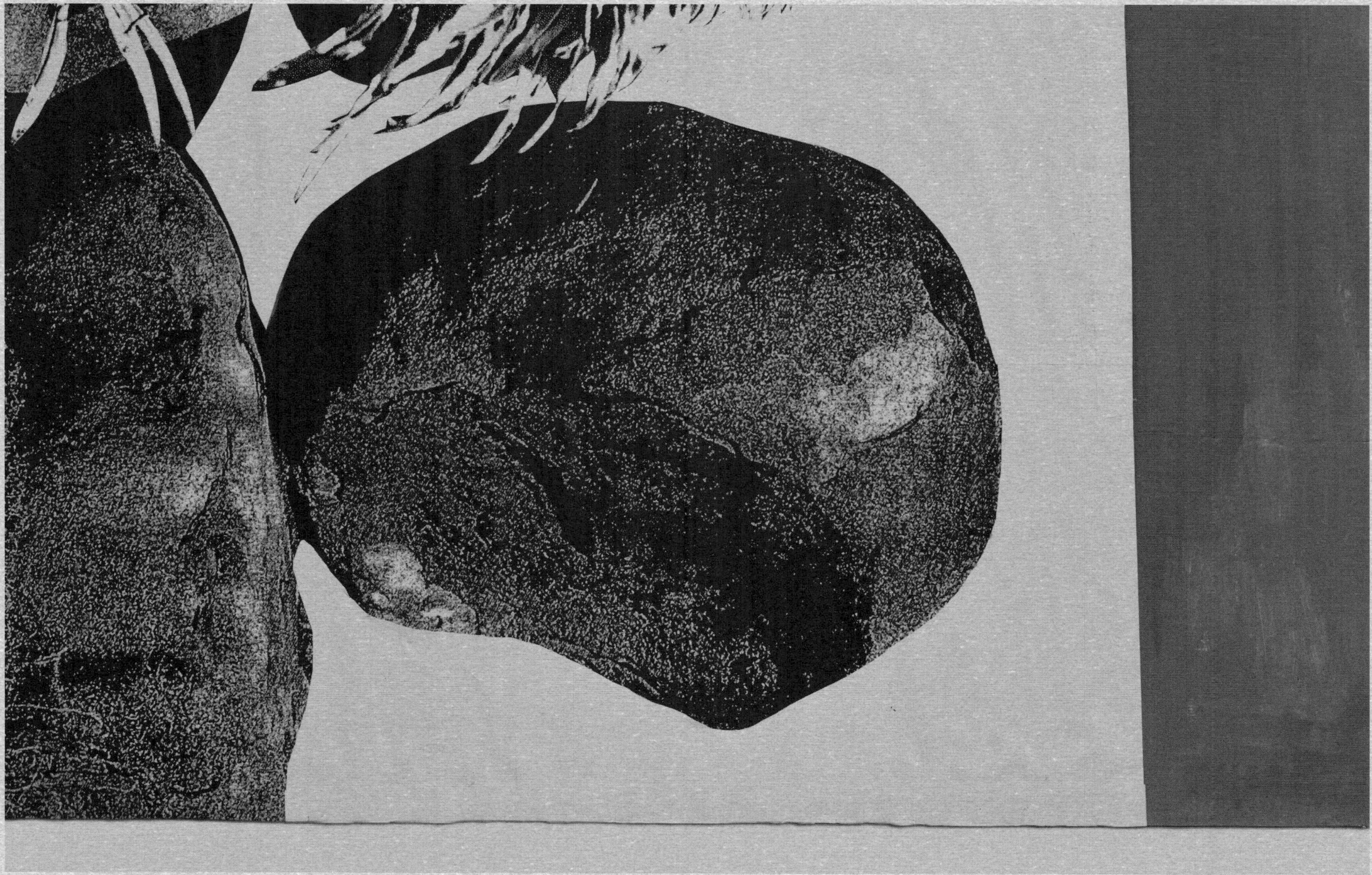

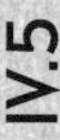
IV.5

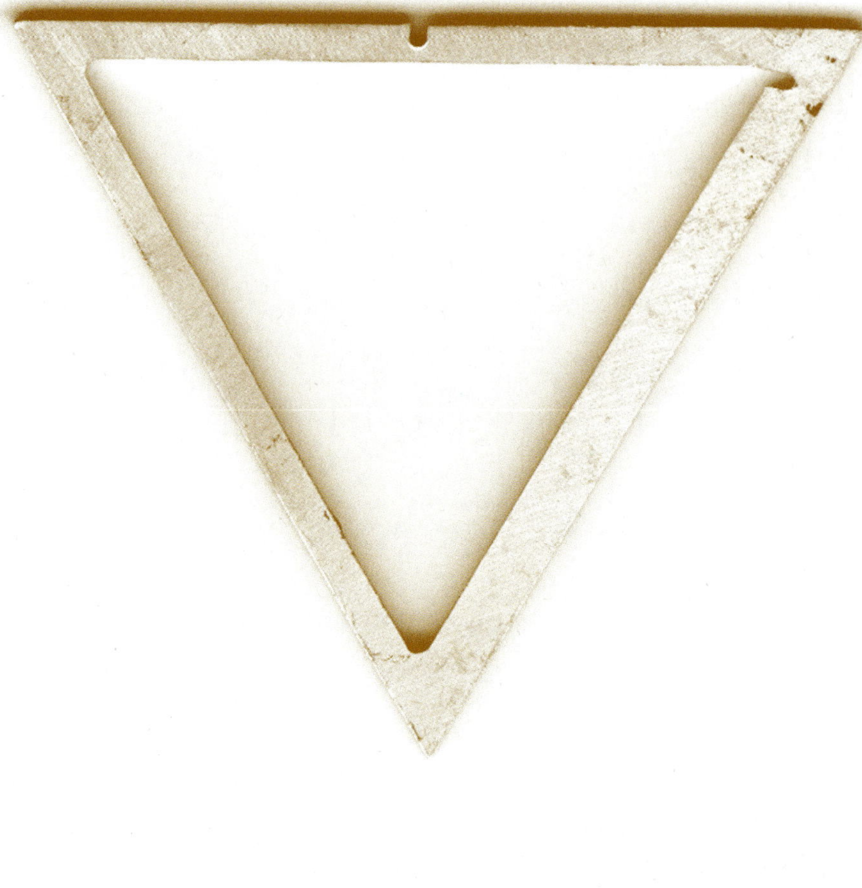

Below Is Air, above Is Material

IV.6

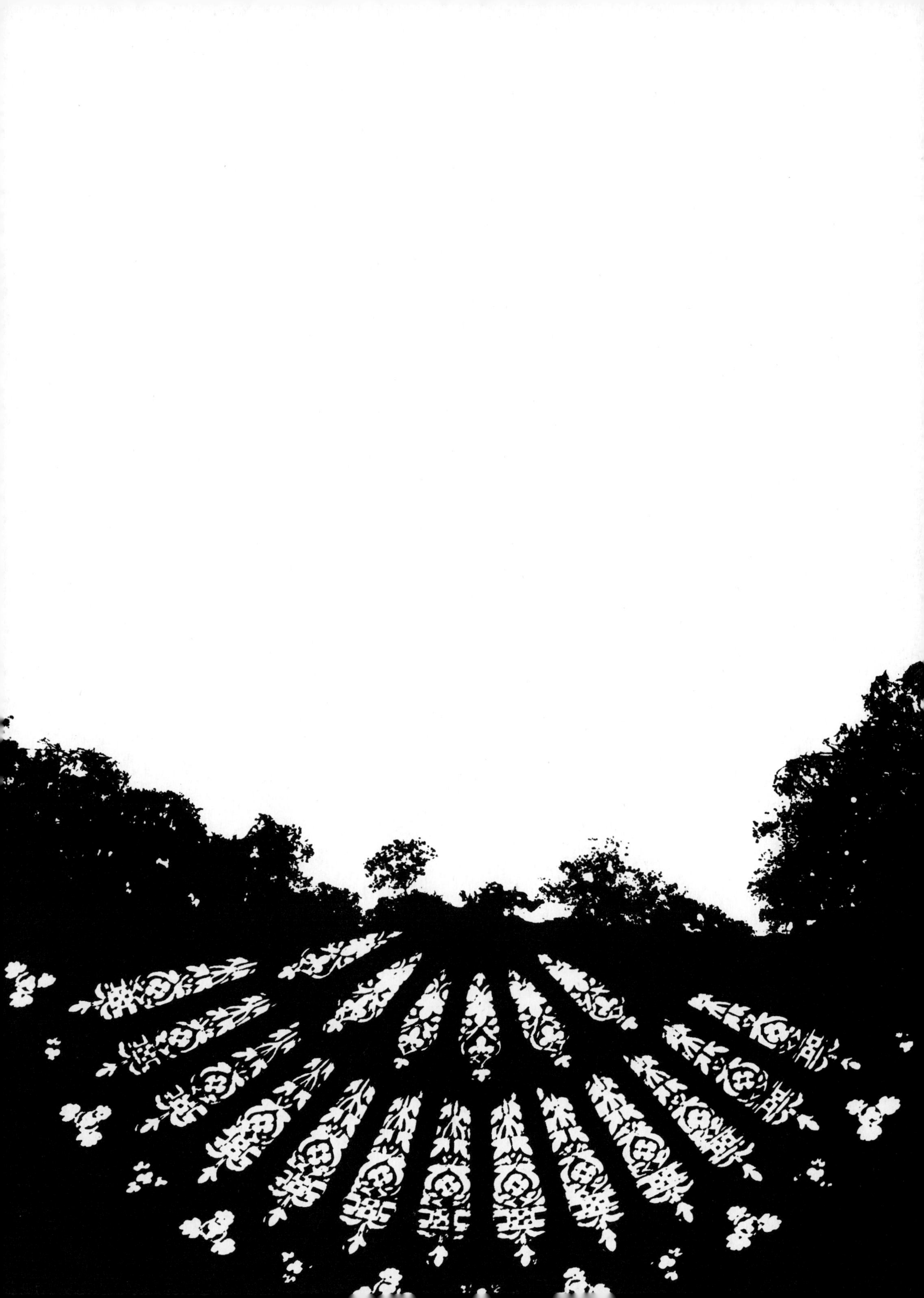

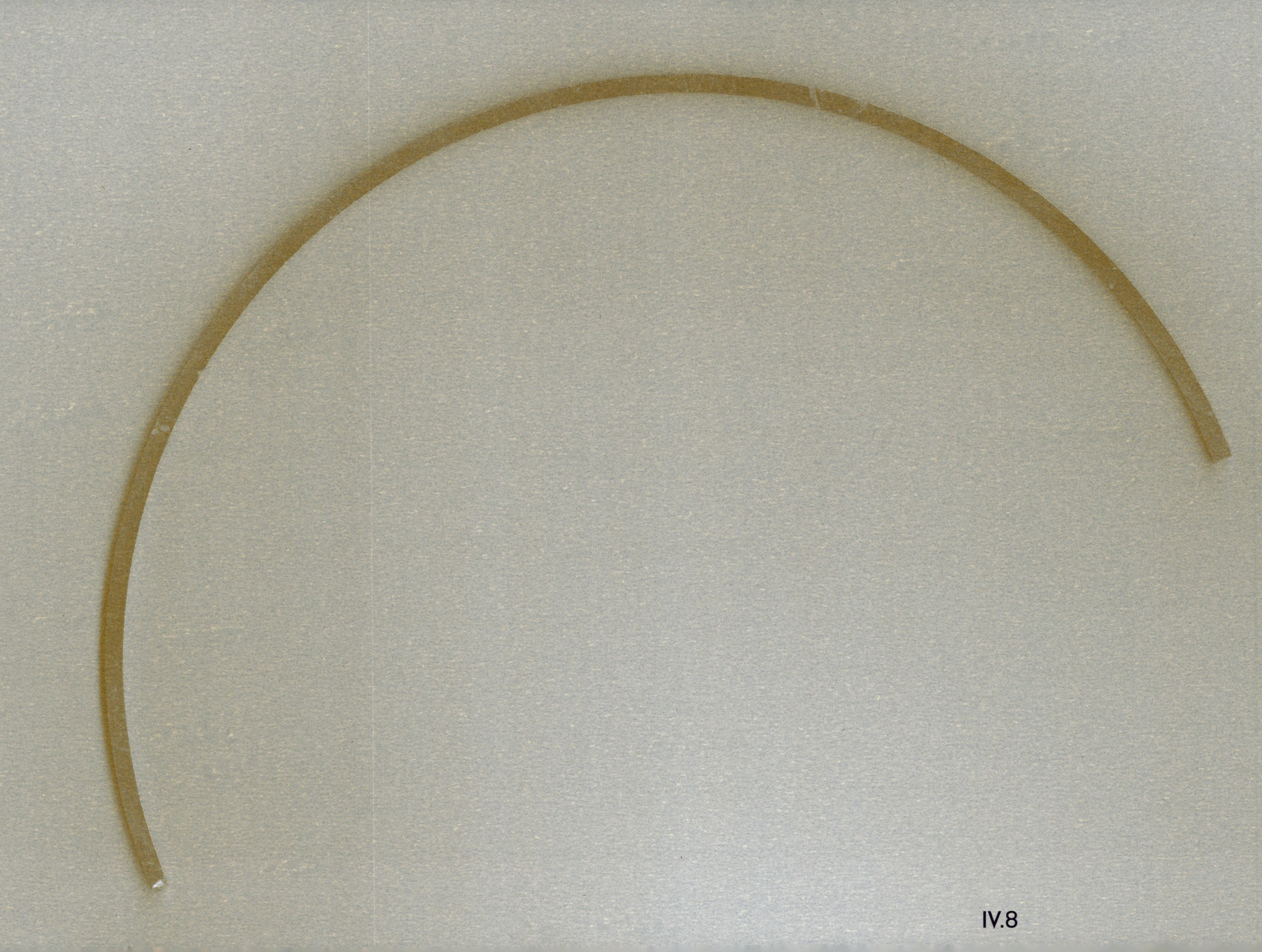

IV.8

Below Is Material, above Is Fear

V.2

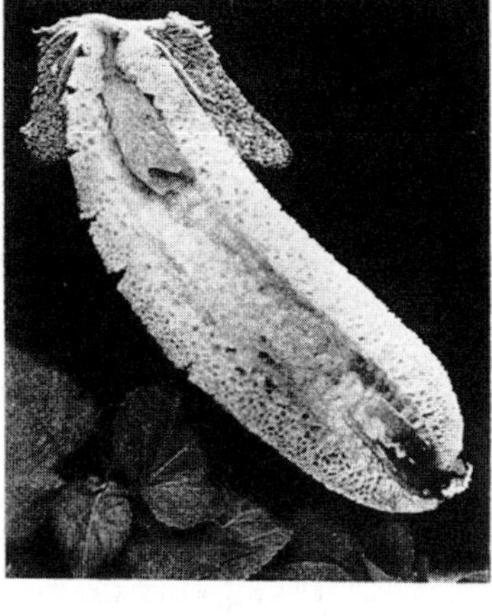

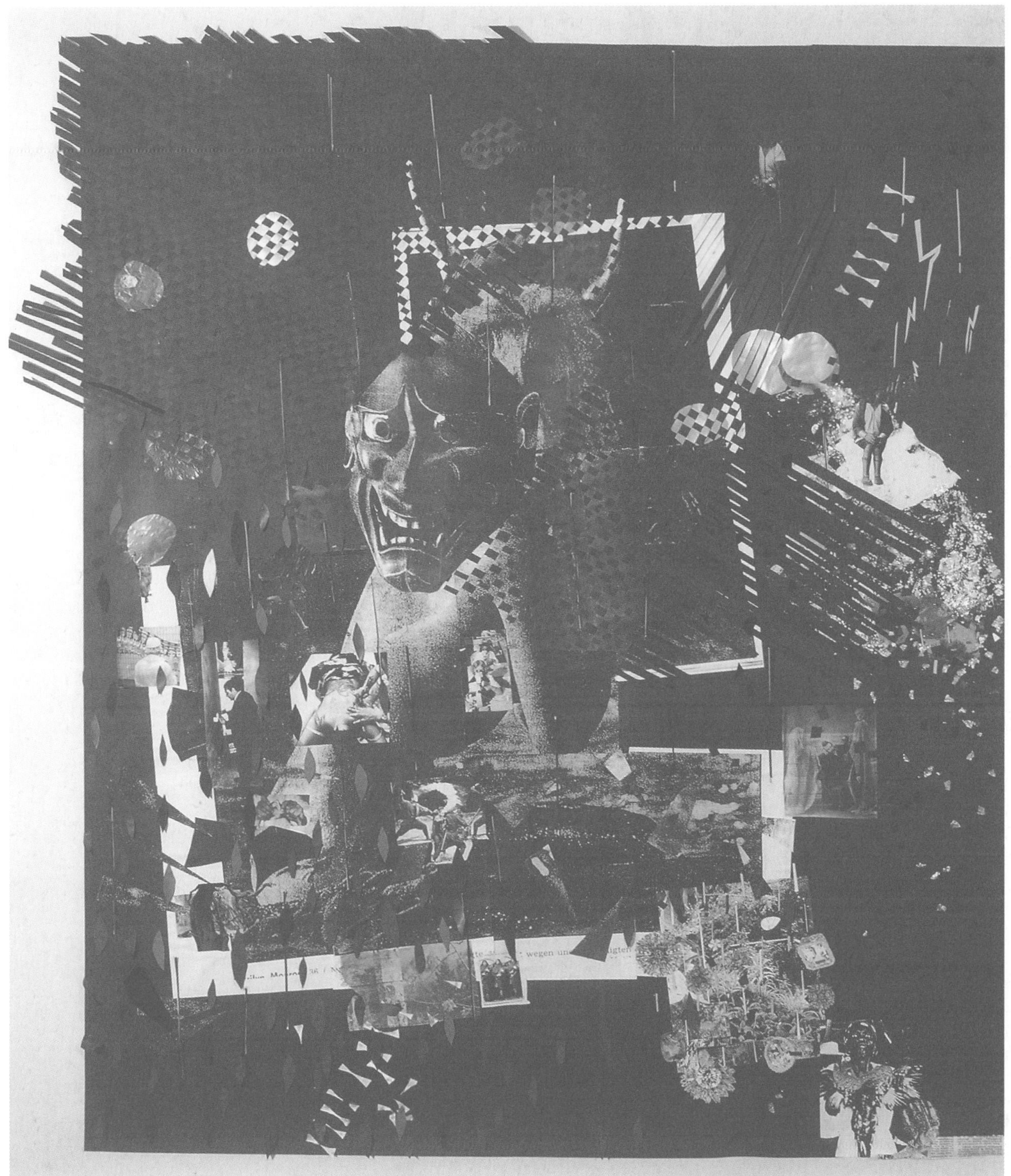

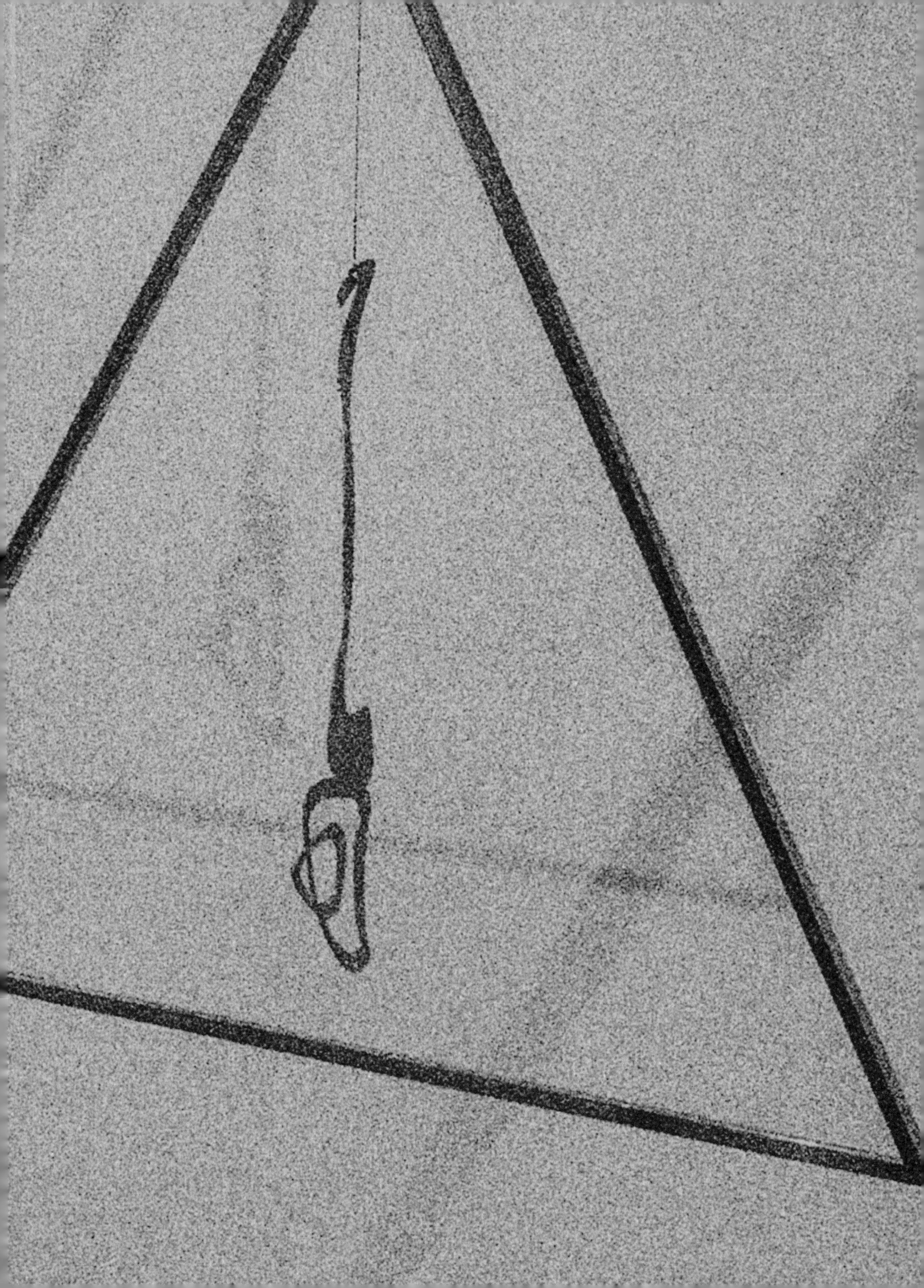

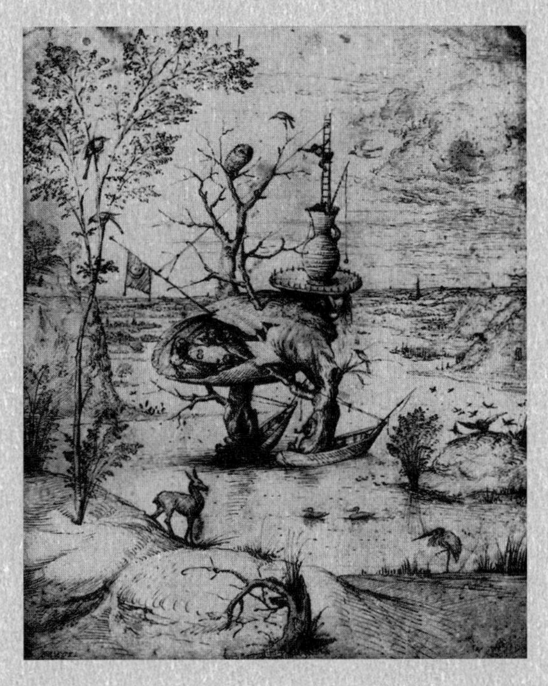

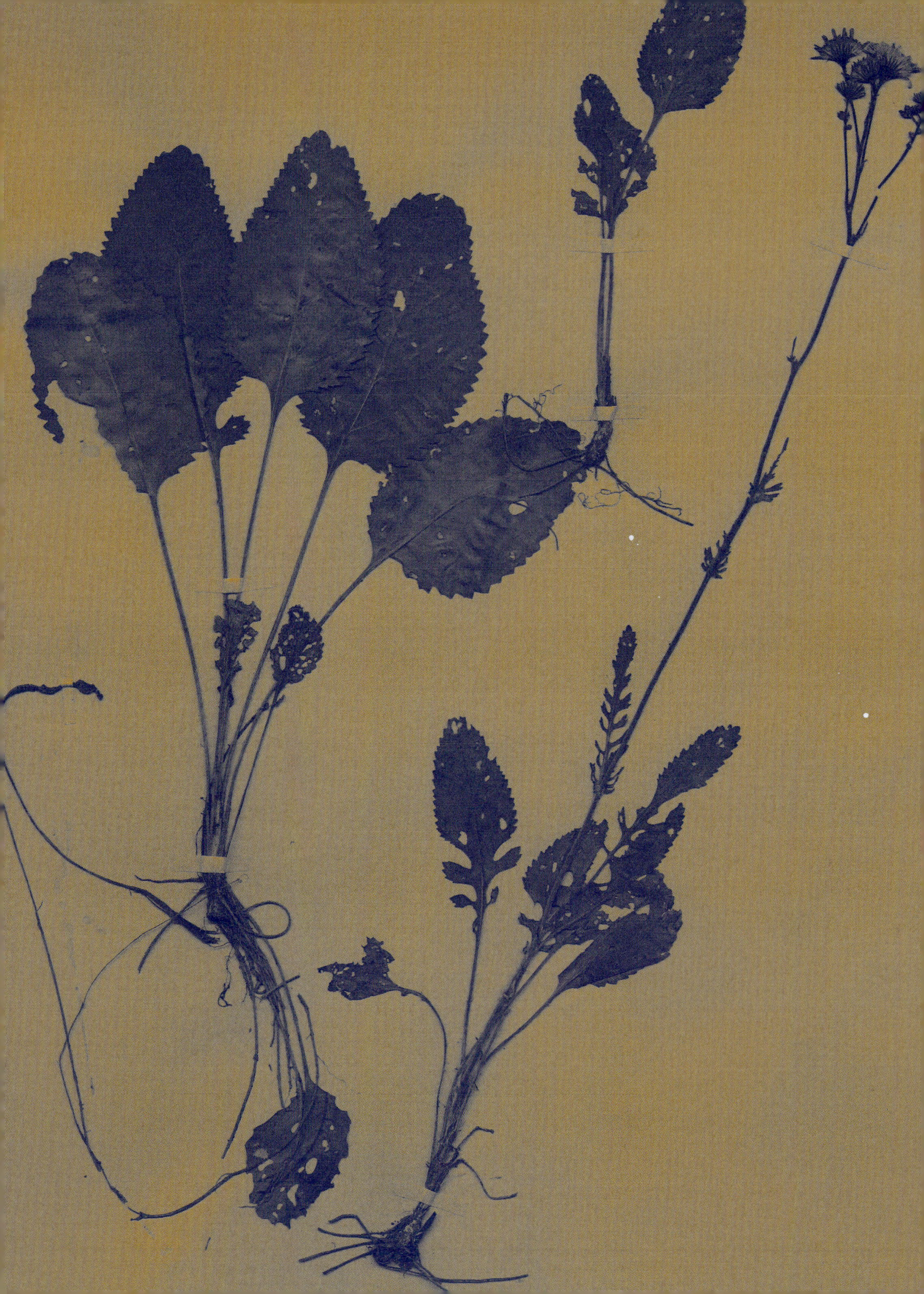

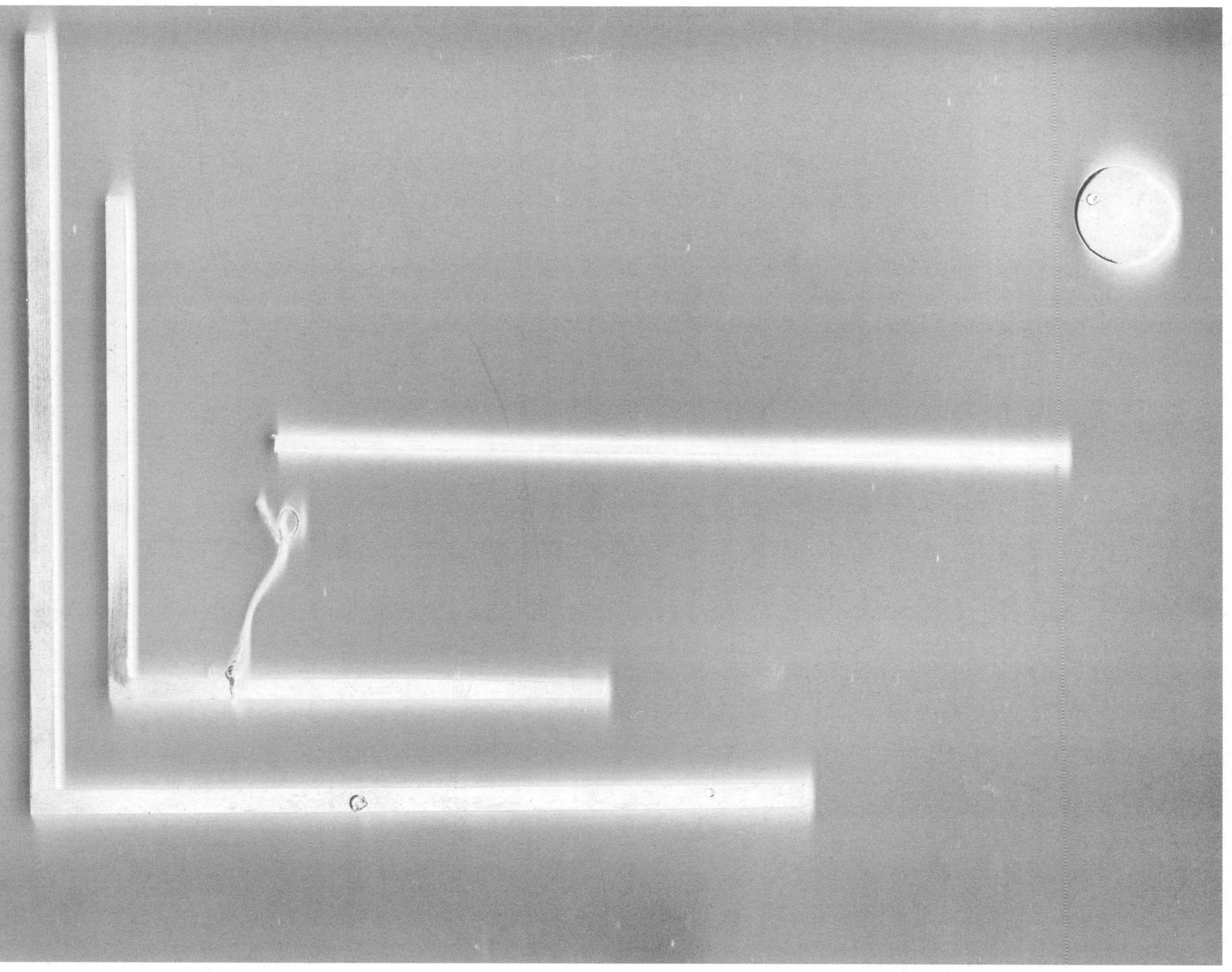

V.7

Below Is Fear, above Is Structure

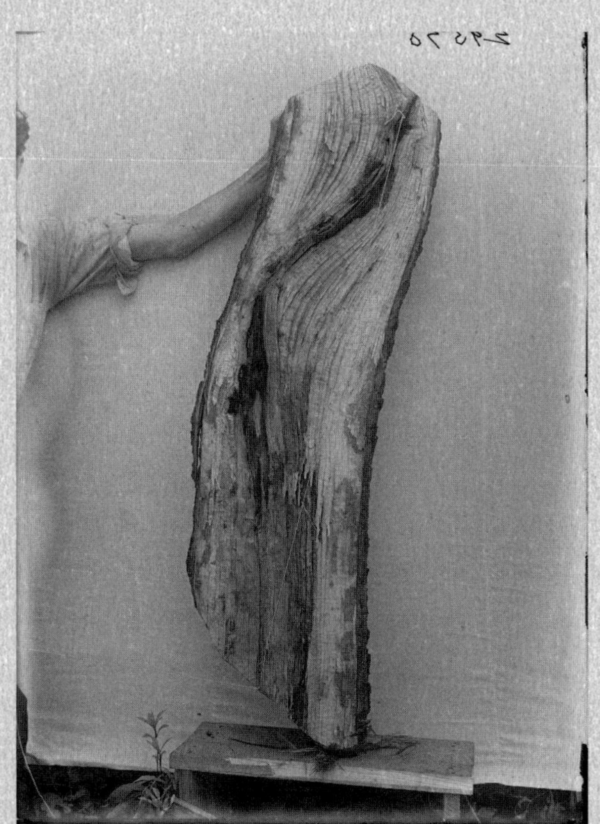

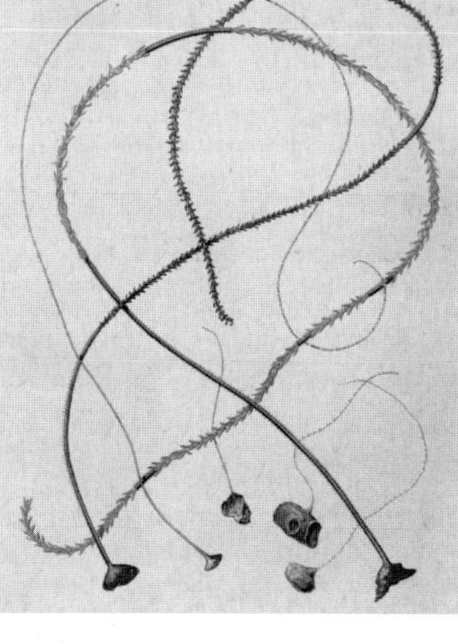

Below Is Structure, above Is Equilibrium

VI.2

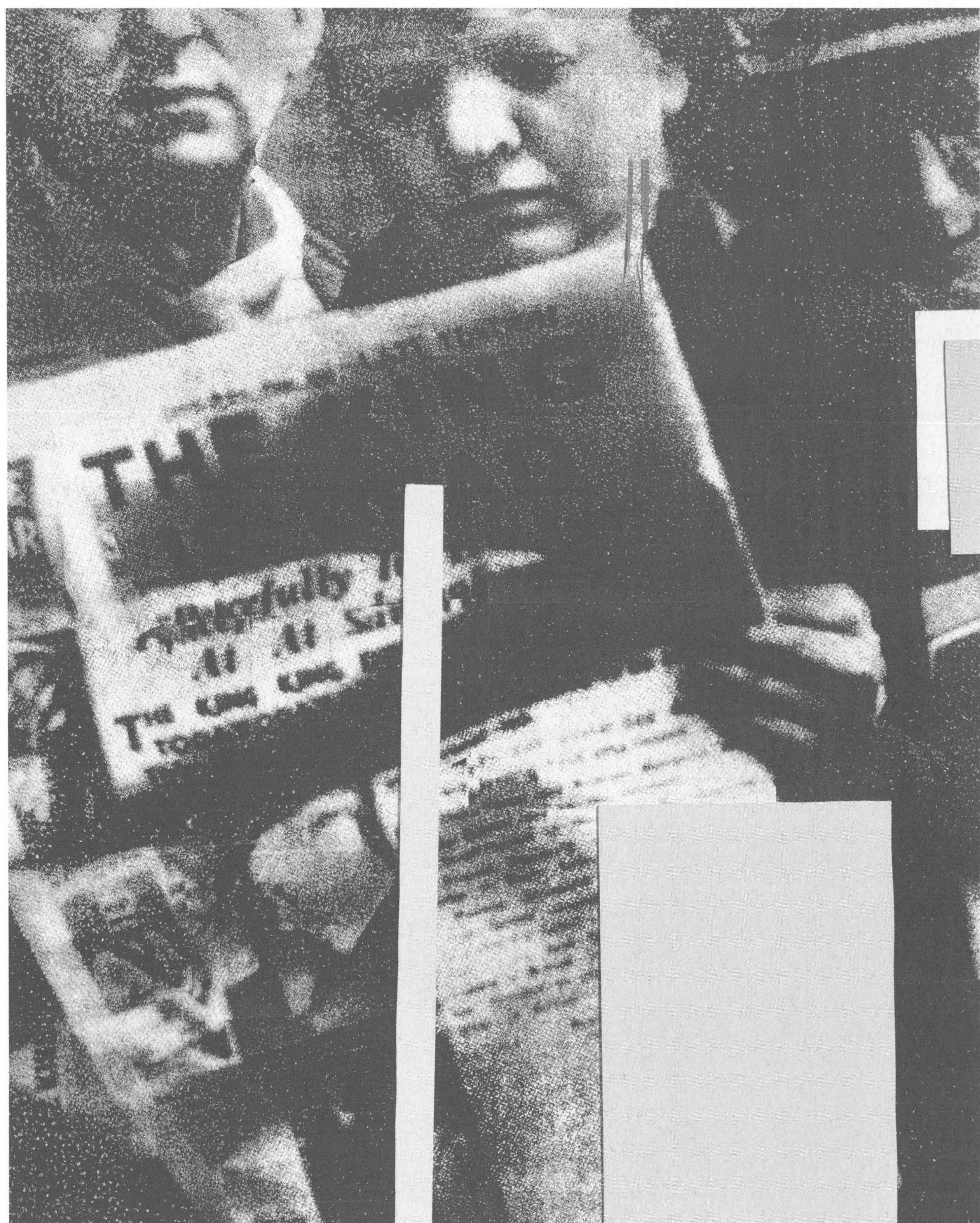

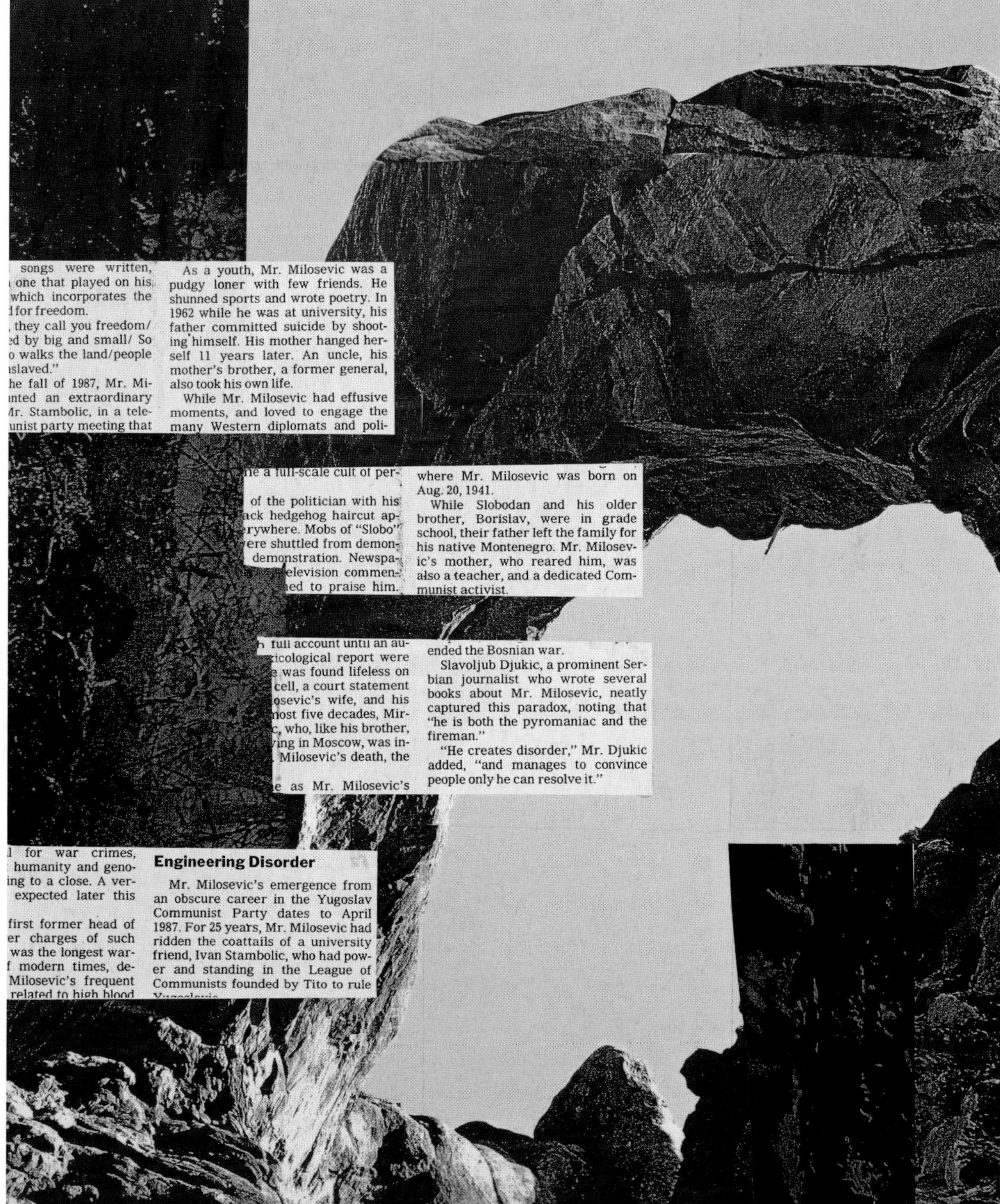

Engineering Disorder

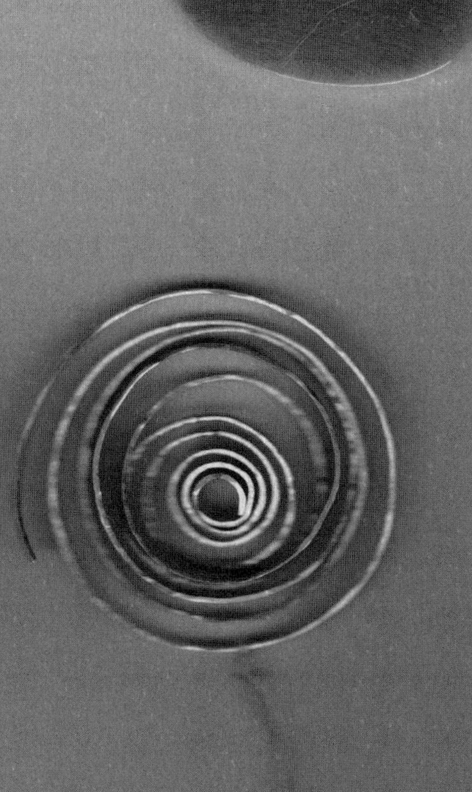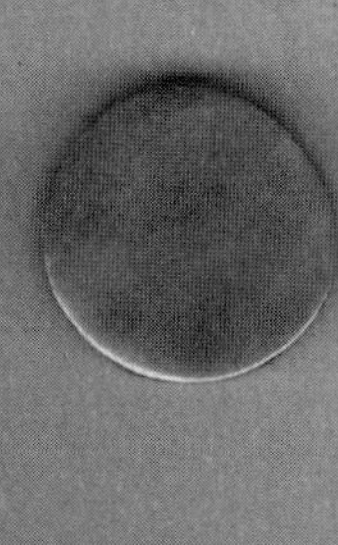

Below Is Equilibrium, above Is Detachment

VI.8

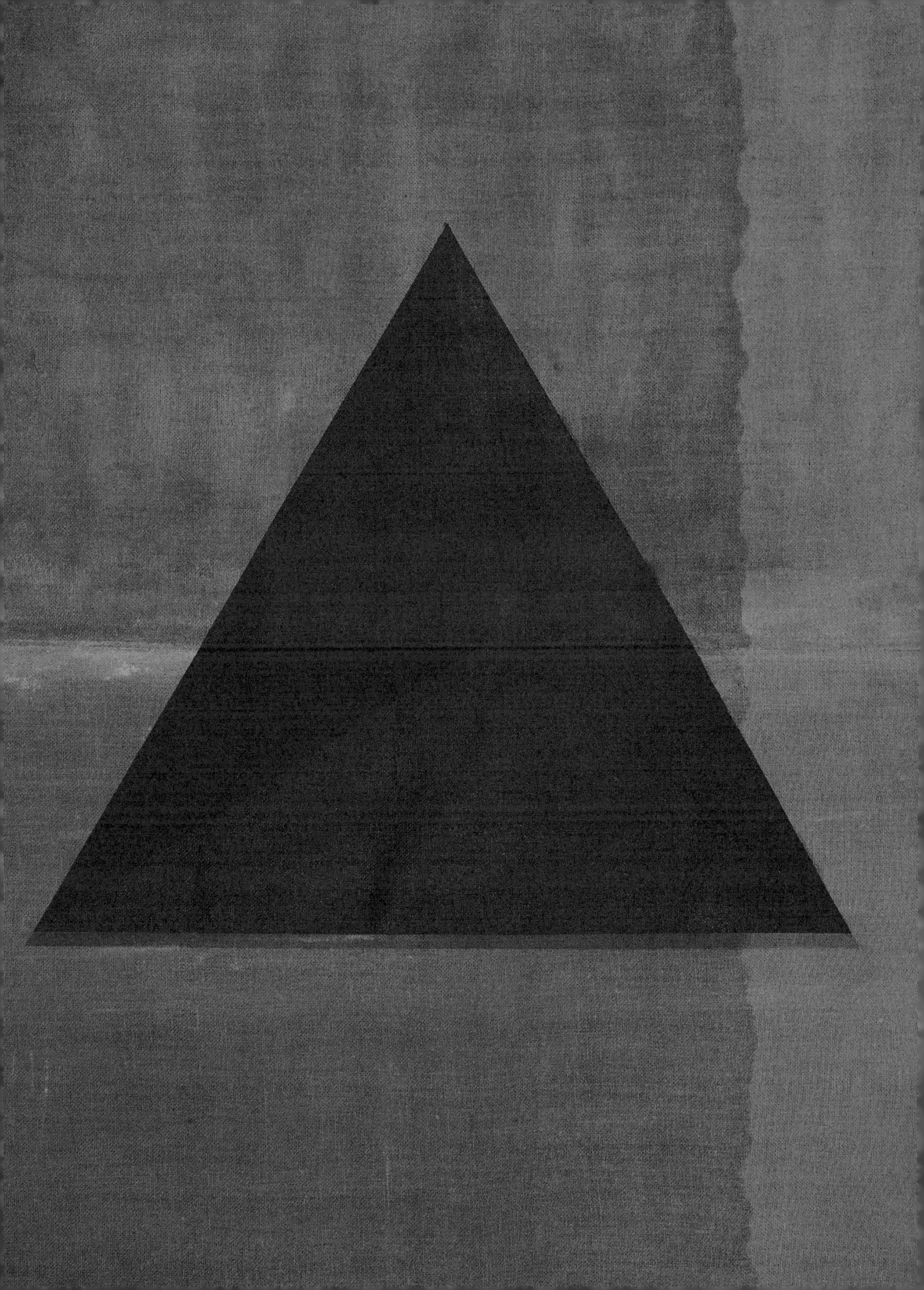

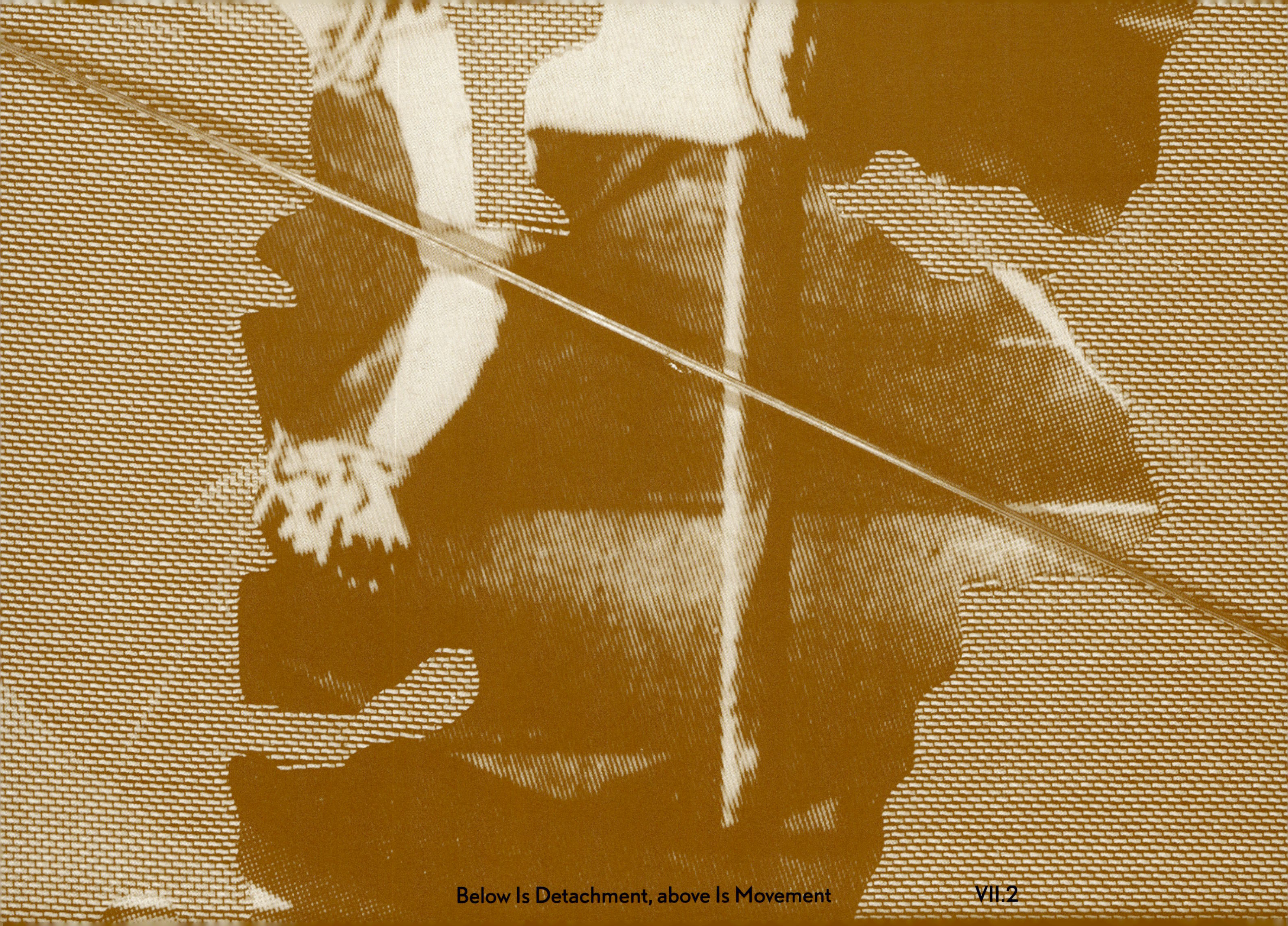

Below Is Detachment, above Is Movement   VII.2

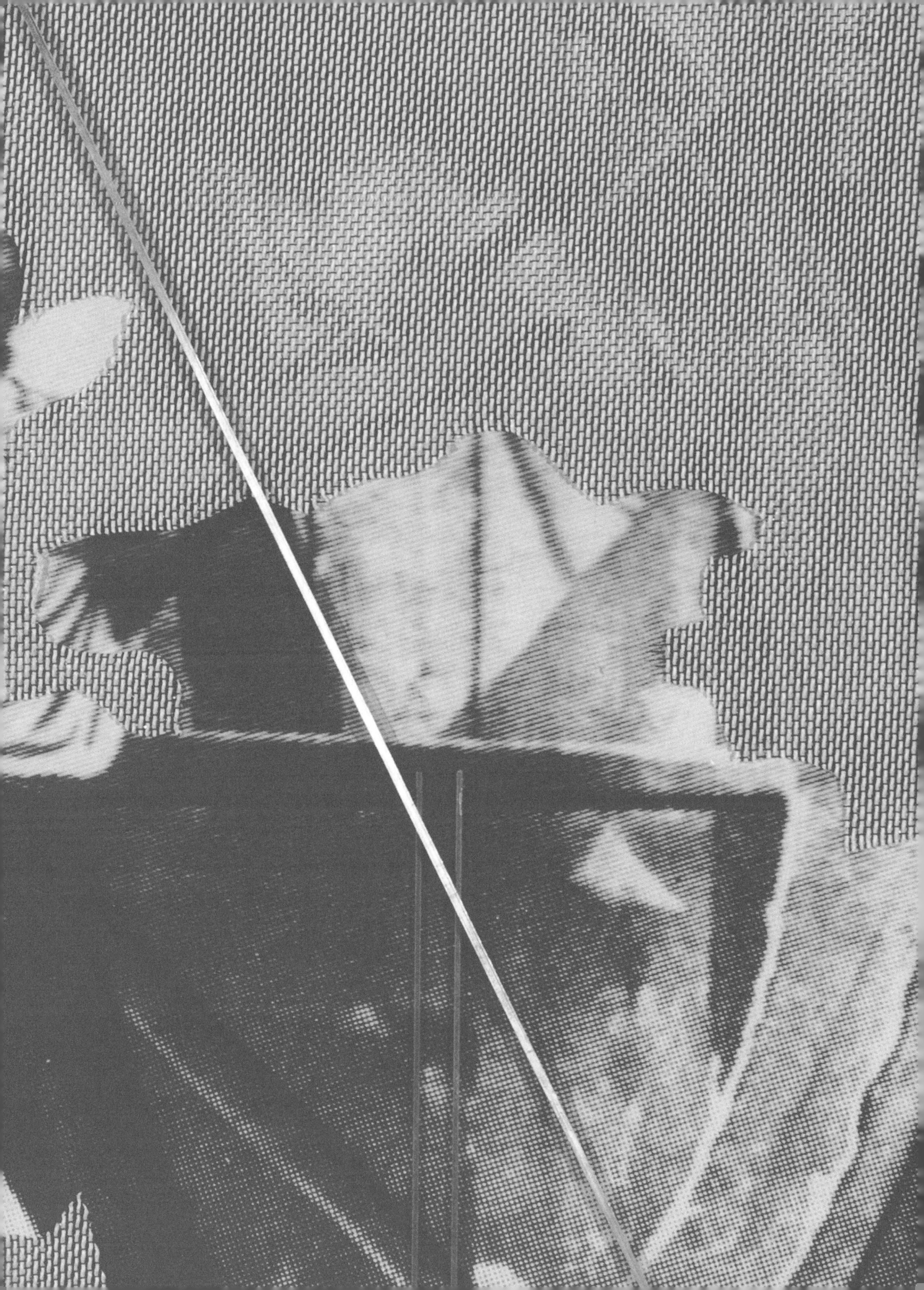

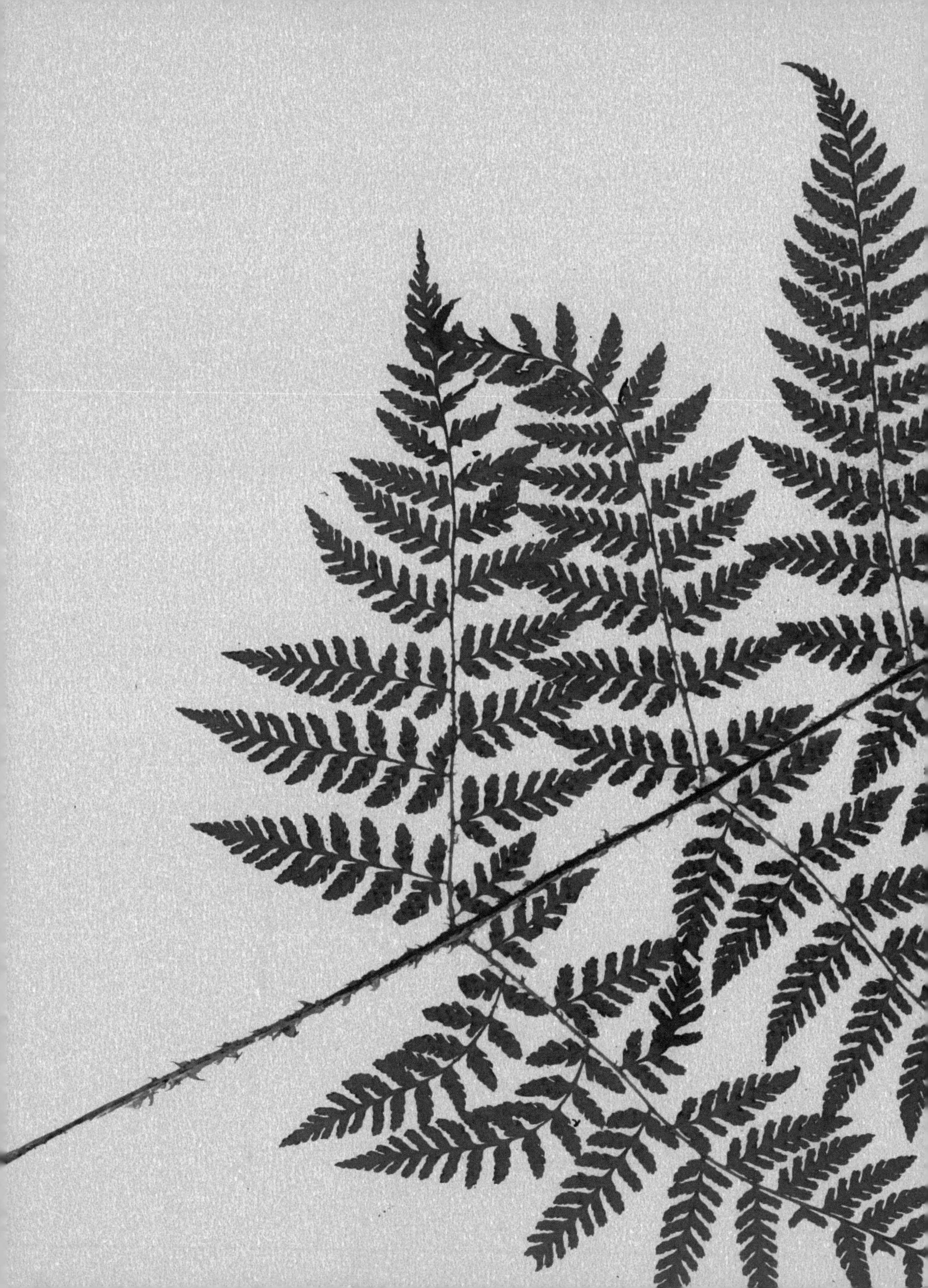

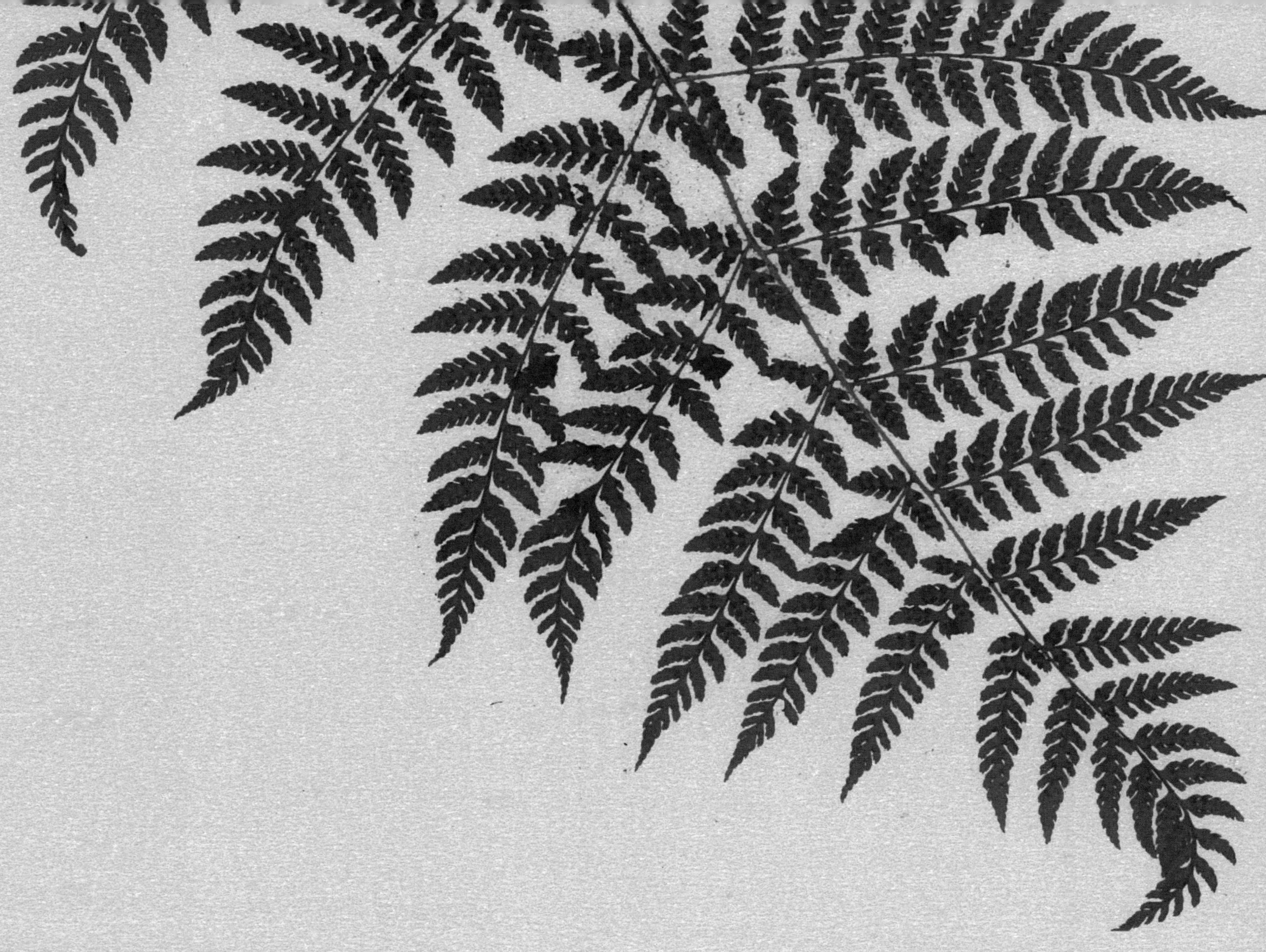

VII.5

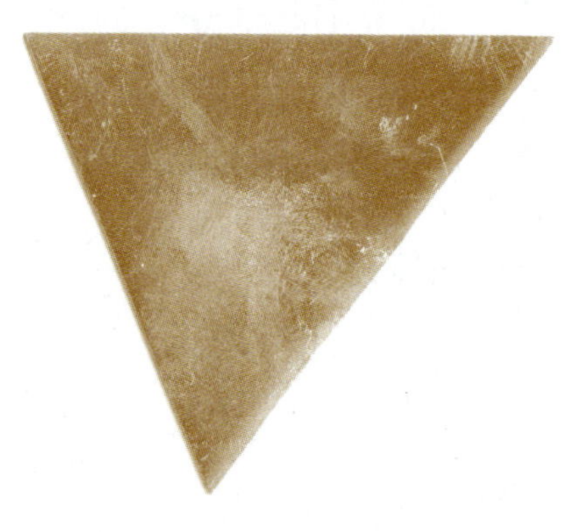

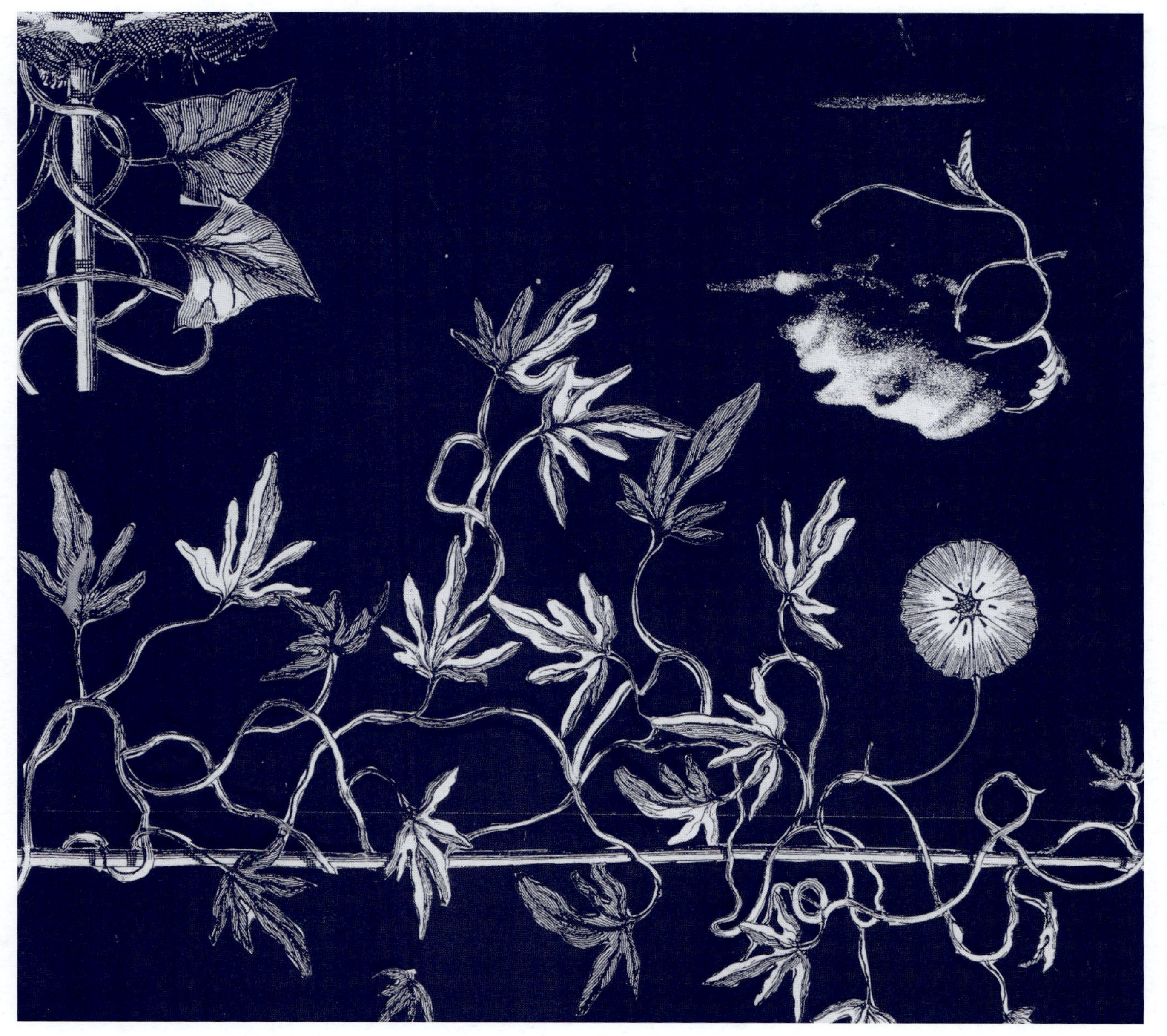

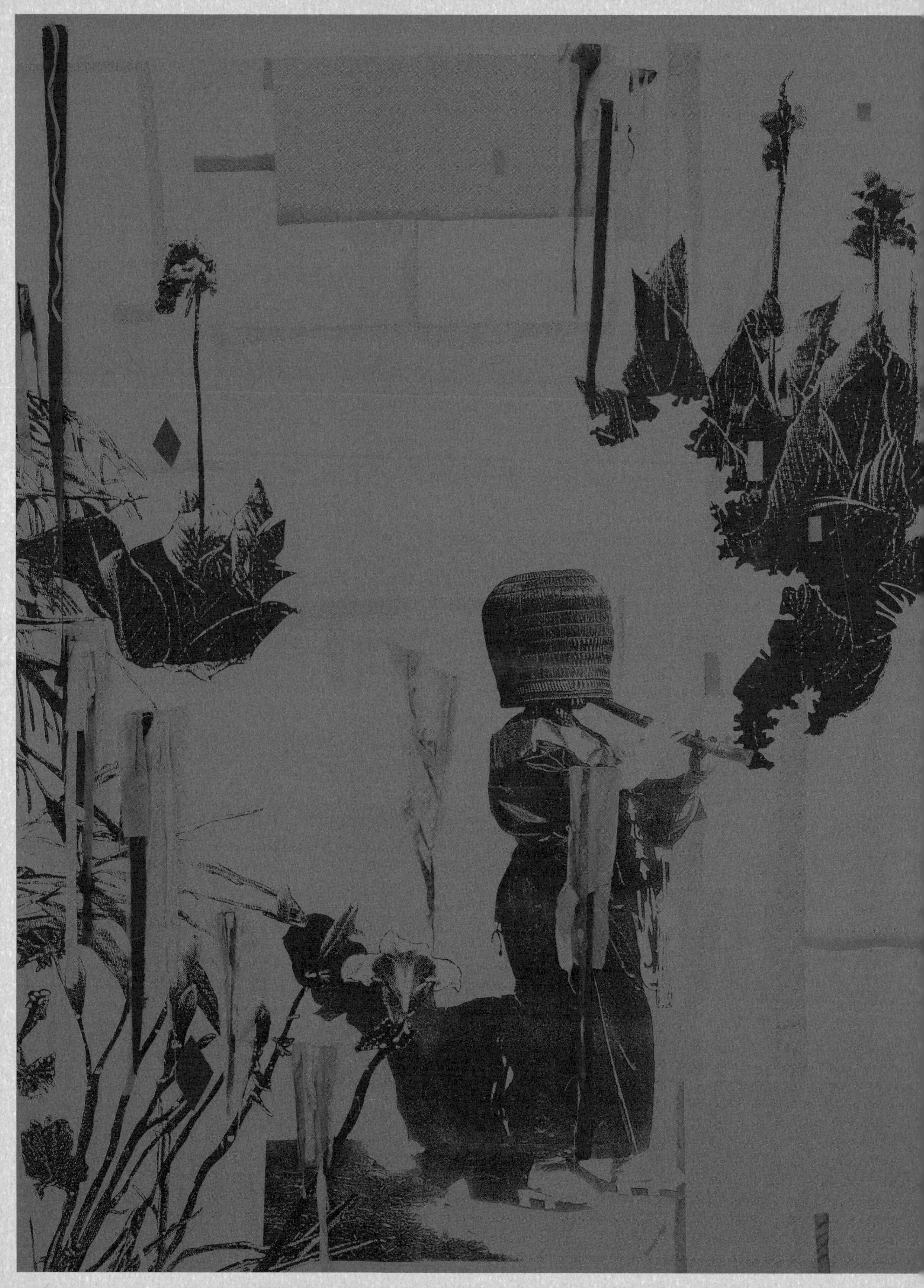

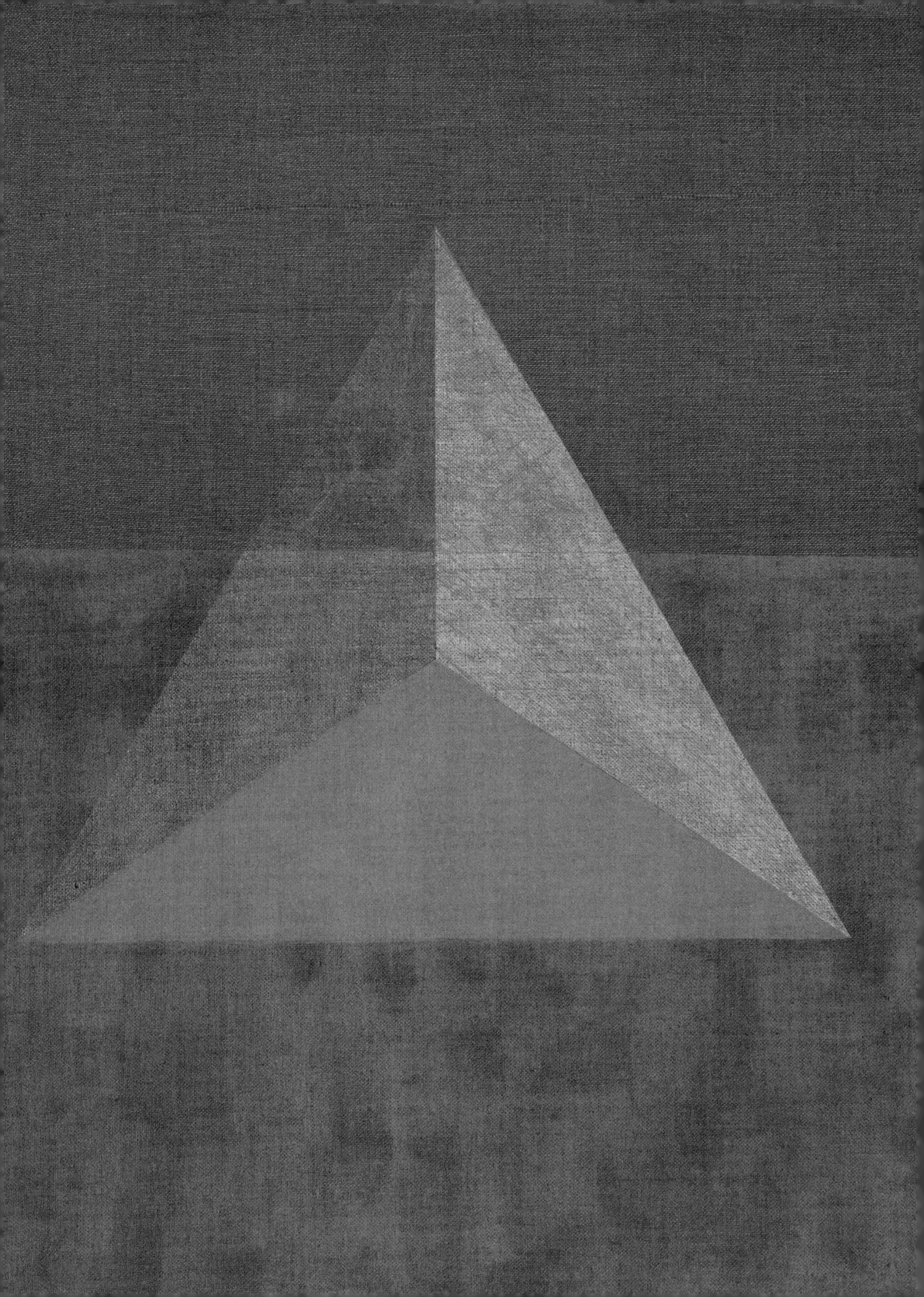

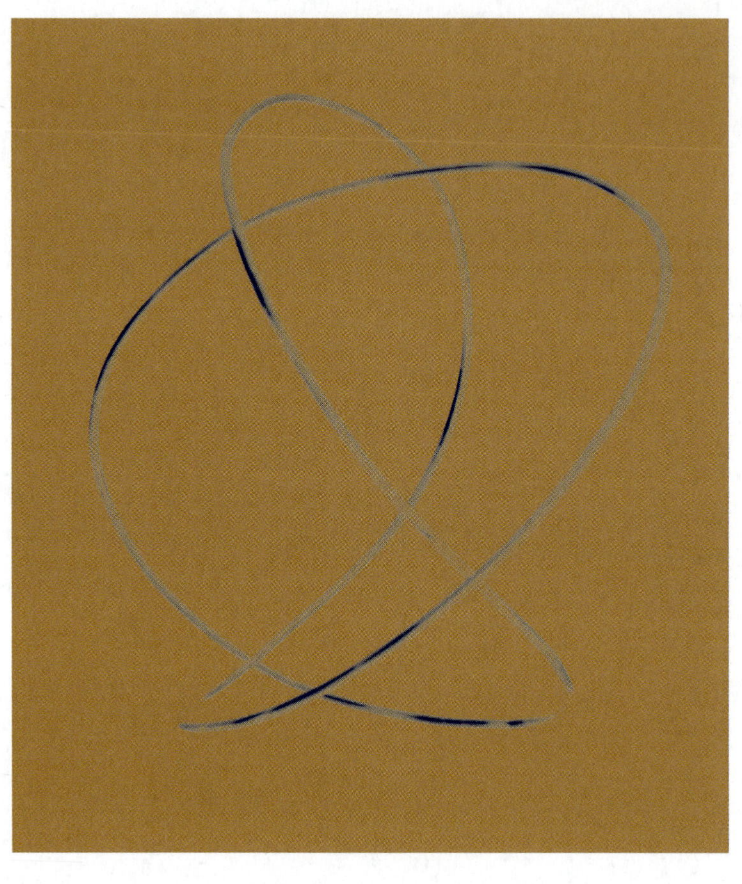

FLOATING

VIII.2

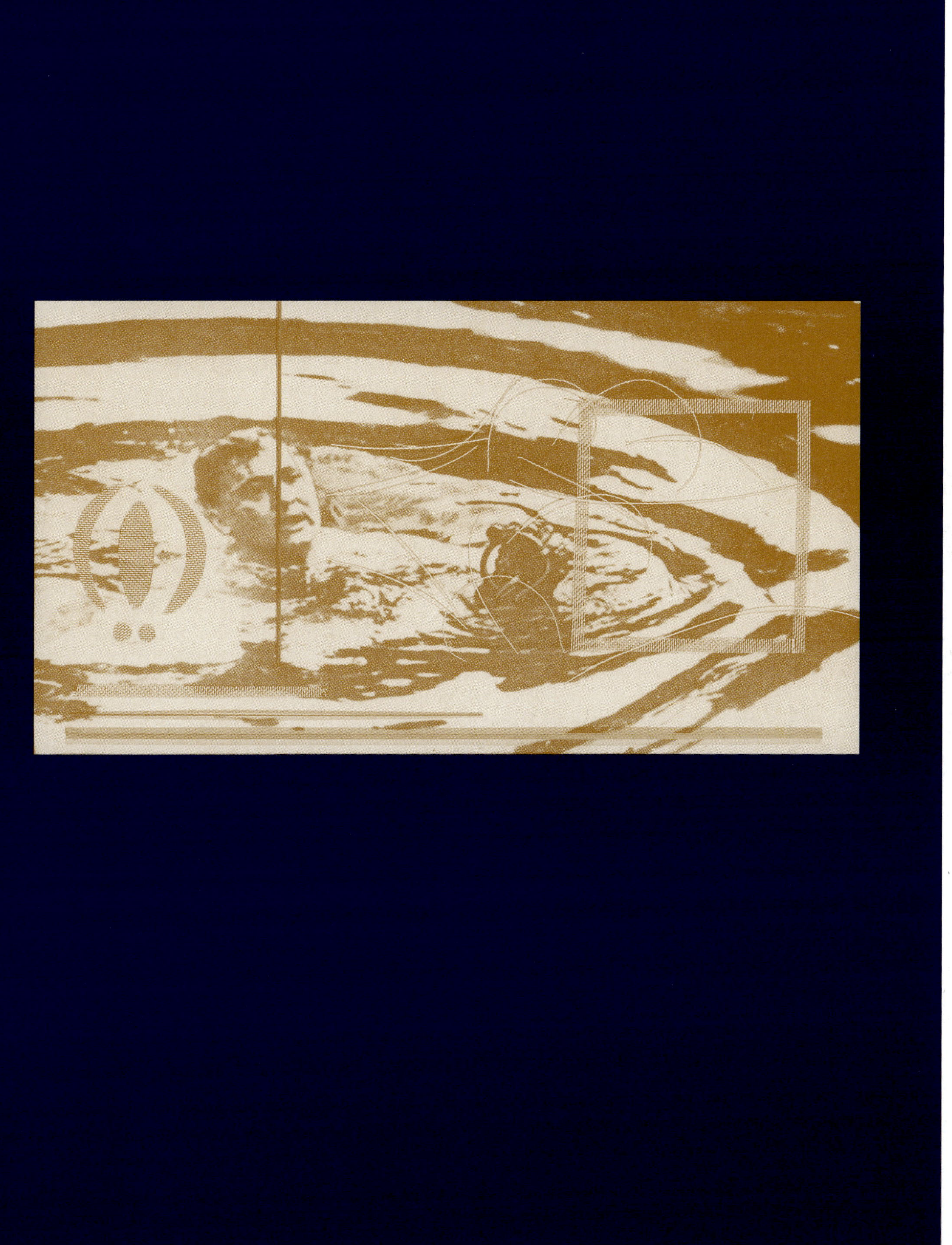

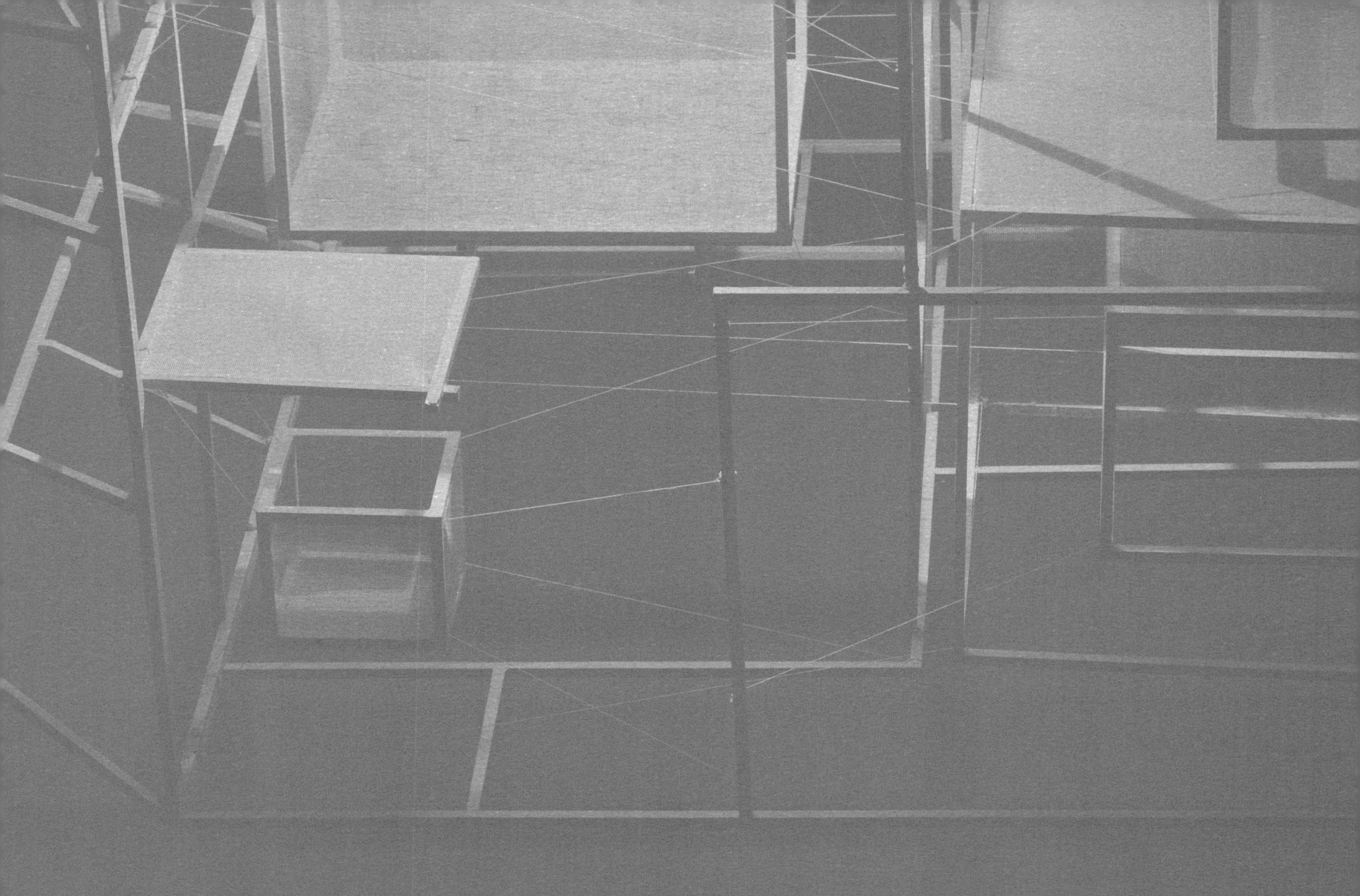

Below Is Excitement, above Is Transformation VIII.4

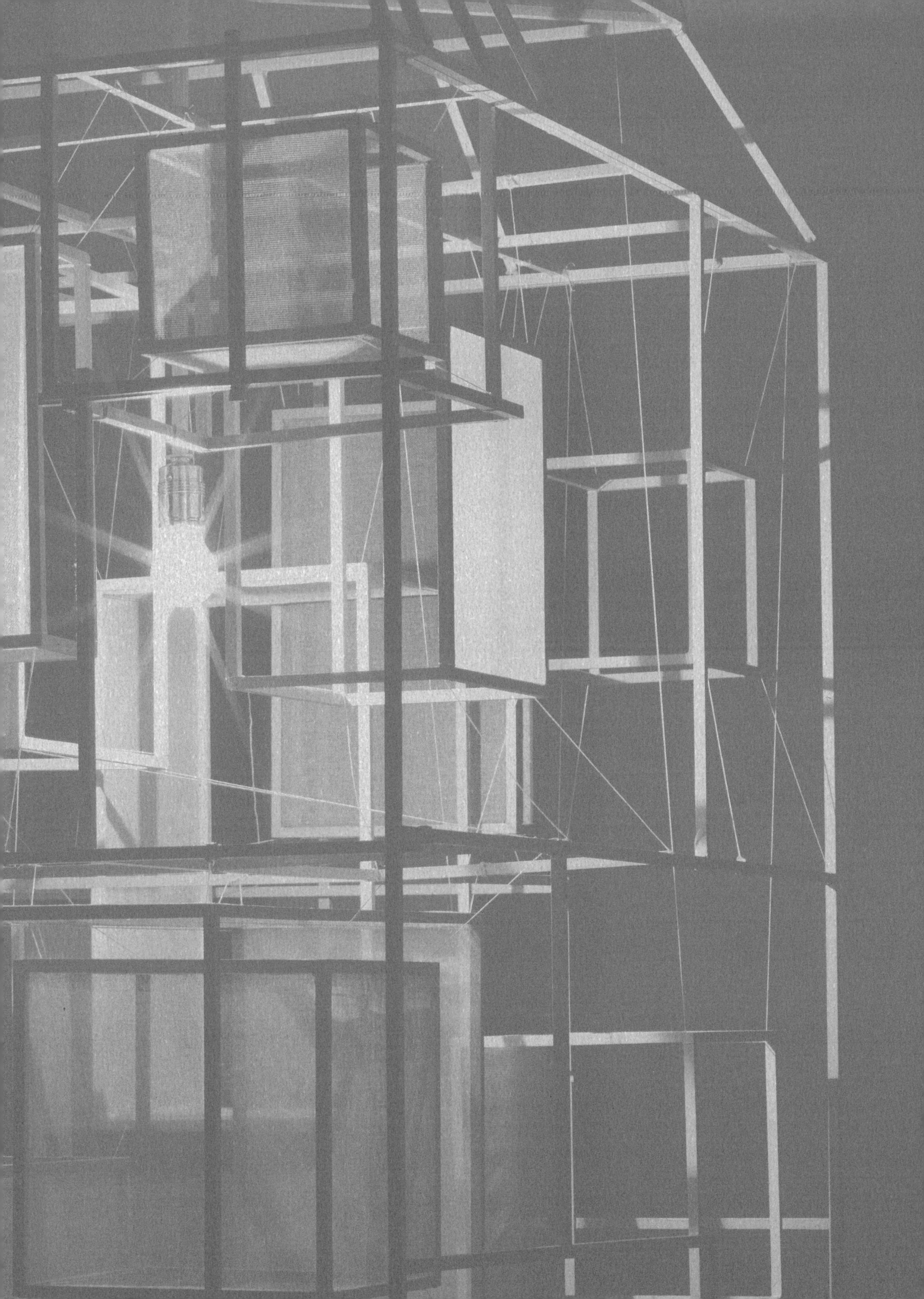

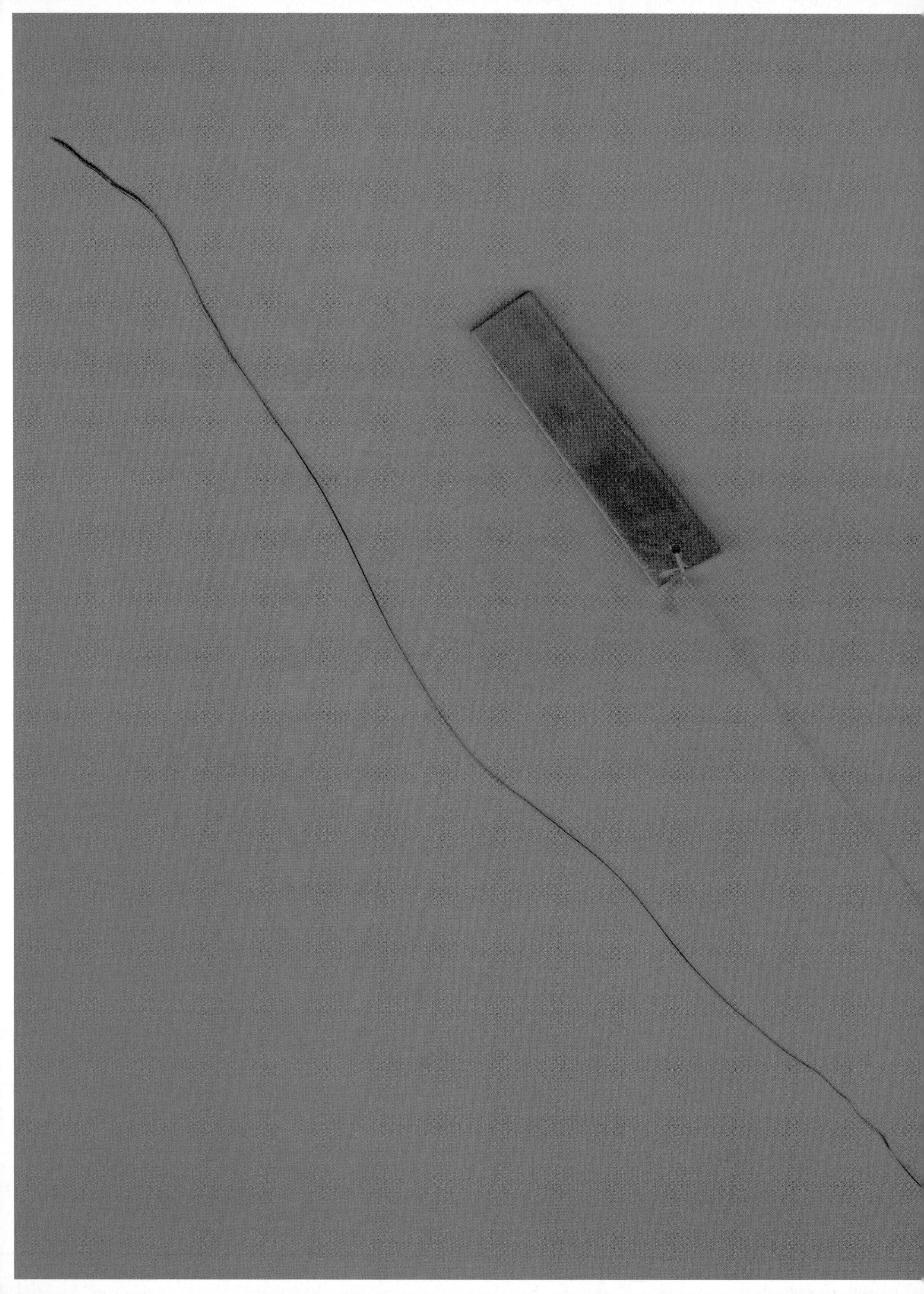

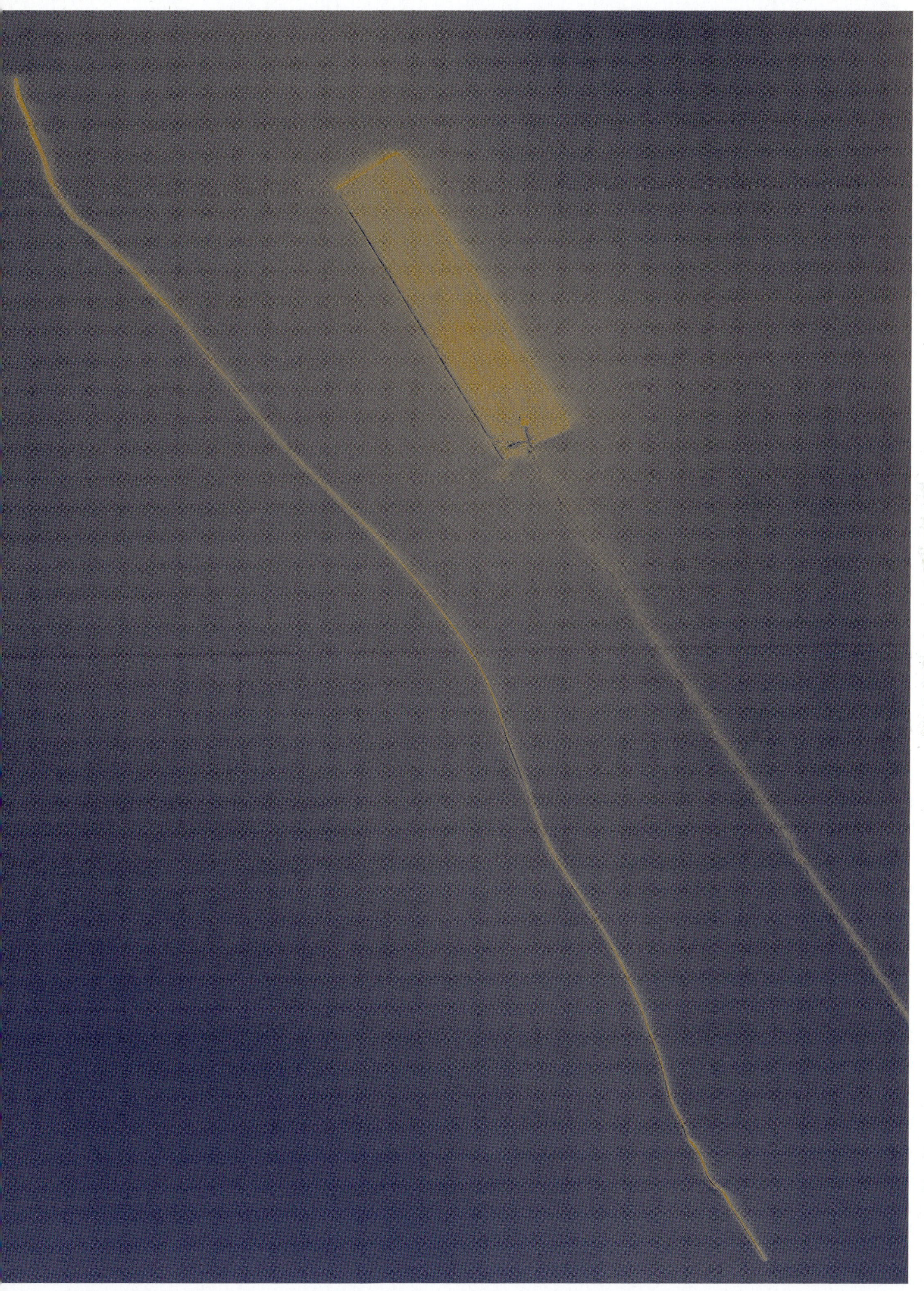

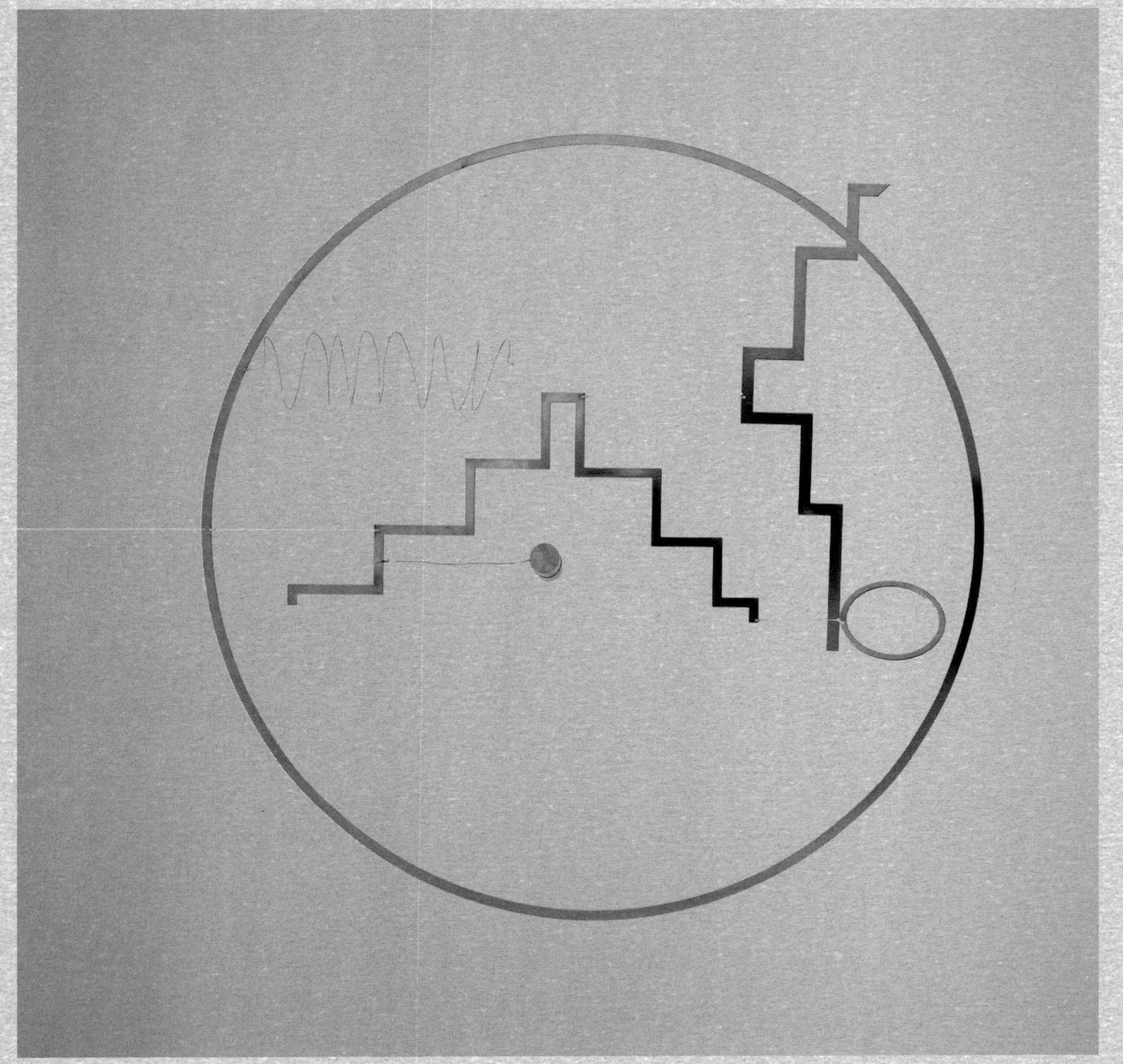

Below Is Transformation, above Is Sorrow

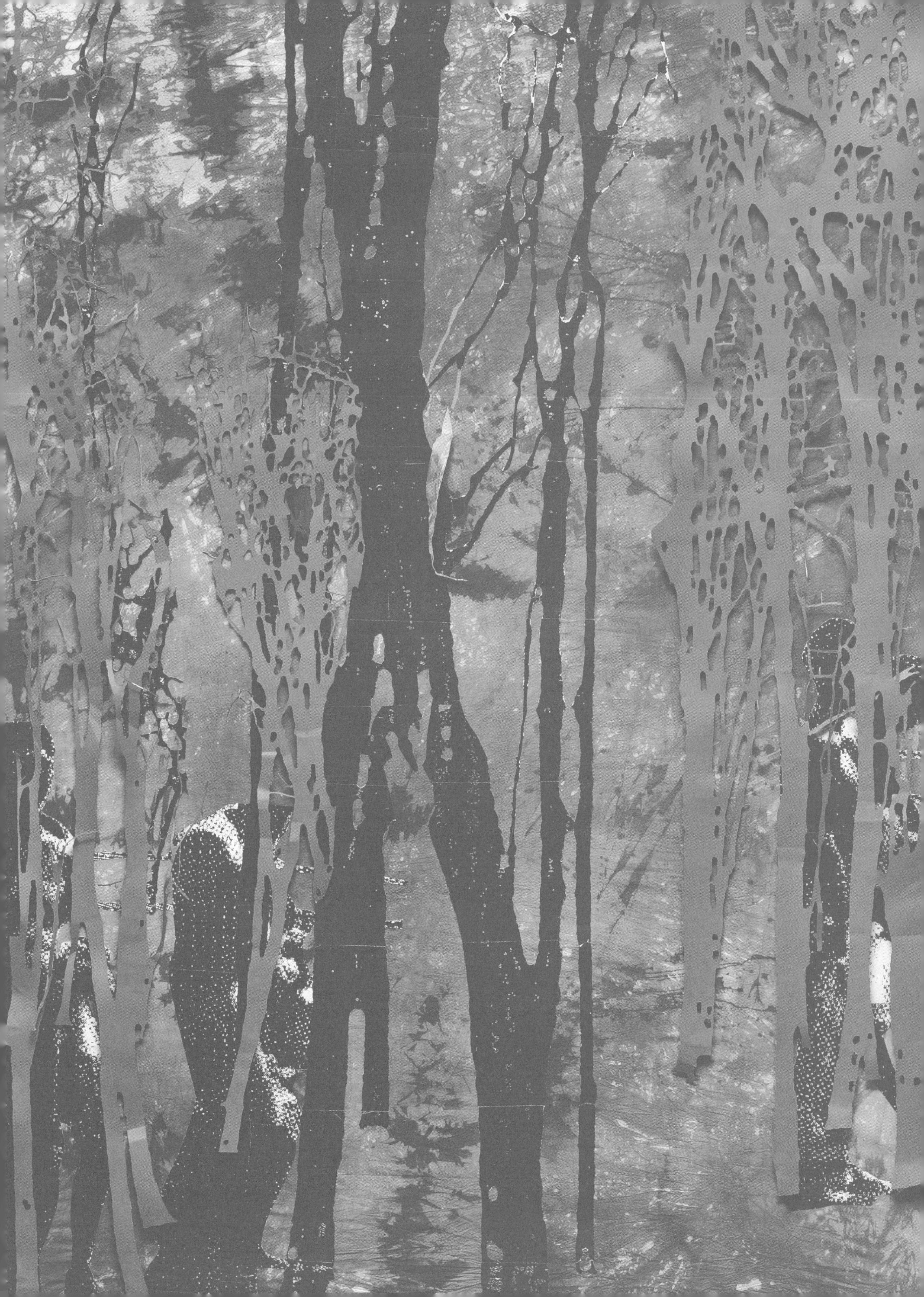

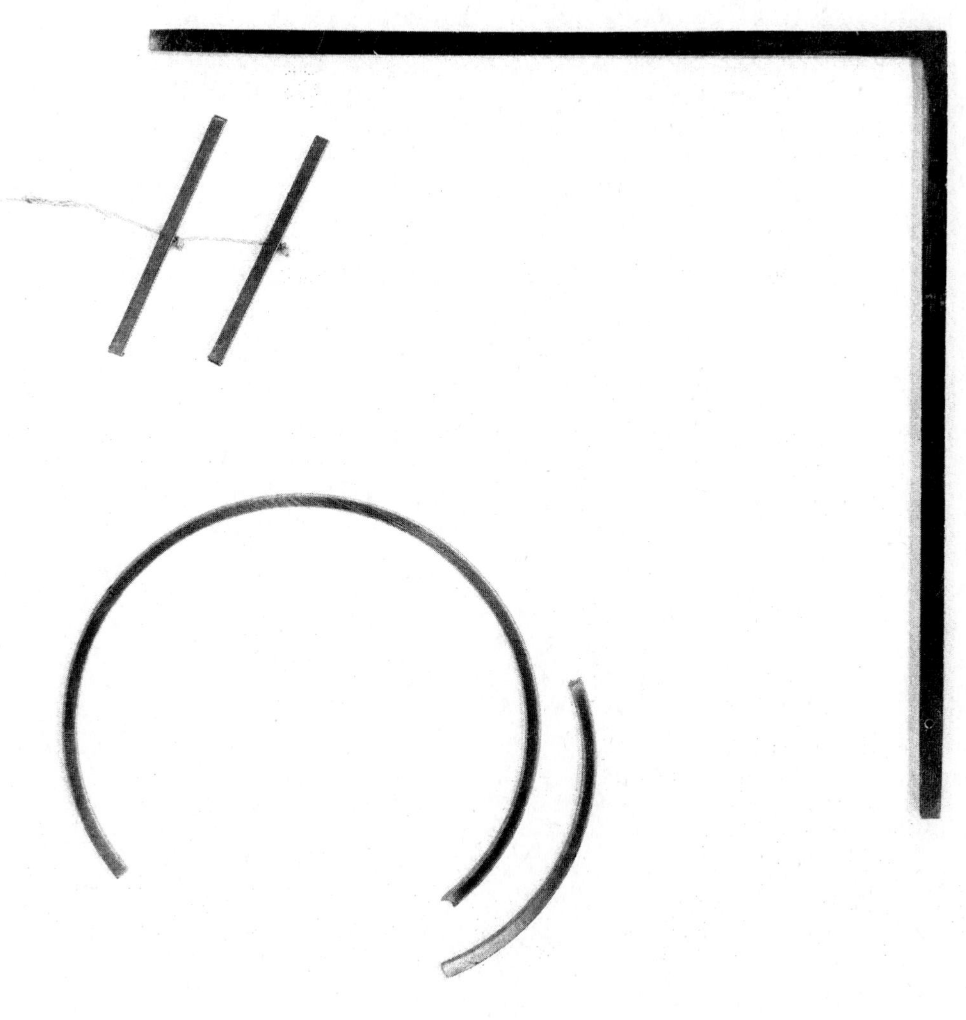

IX.3

Below Is Sorrow, above Is Serenity

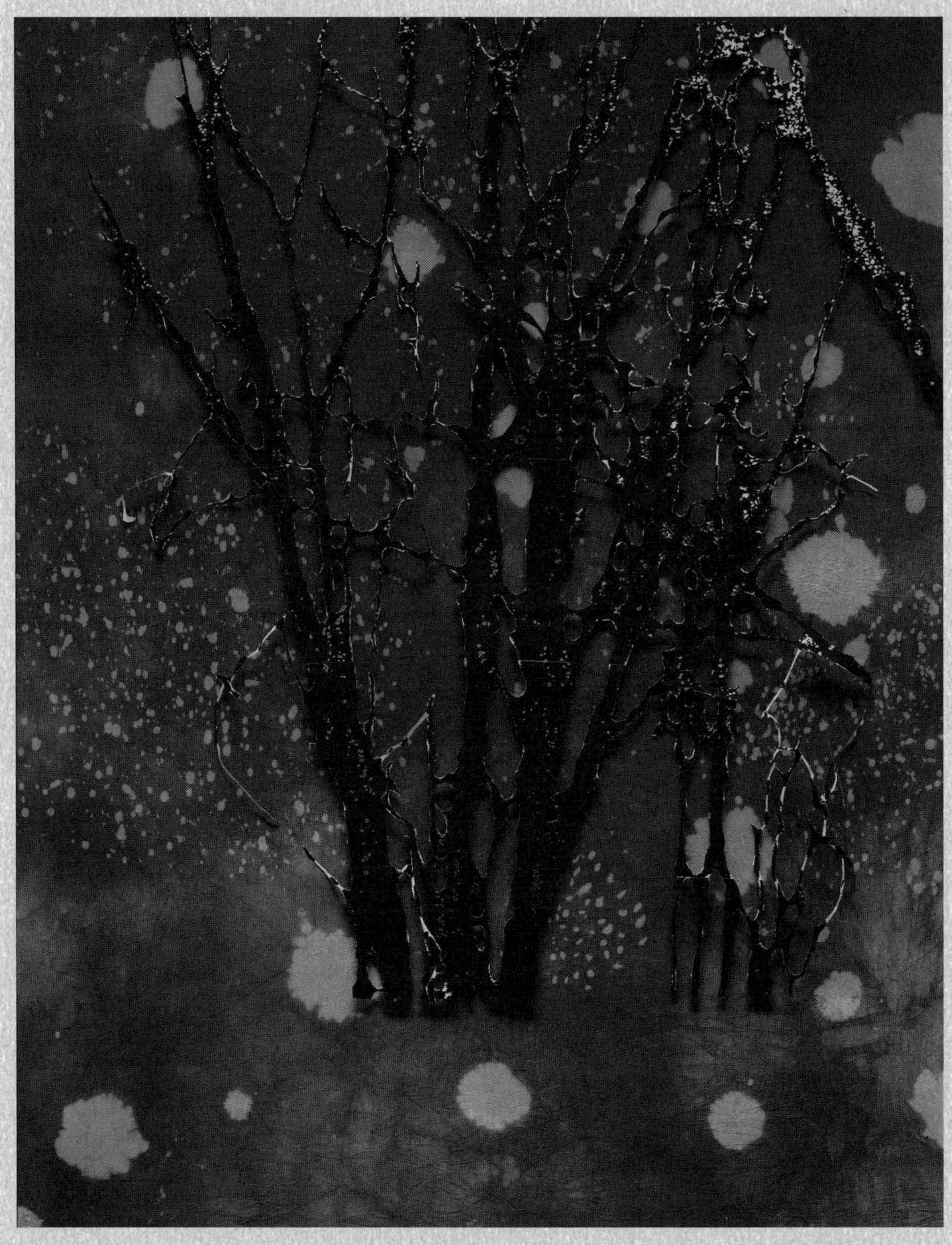

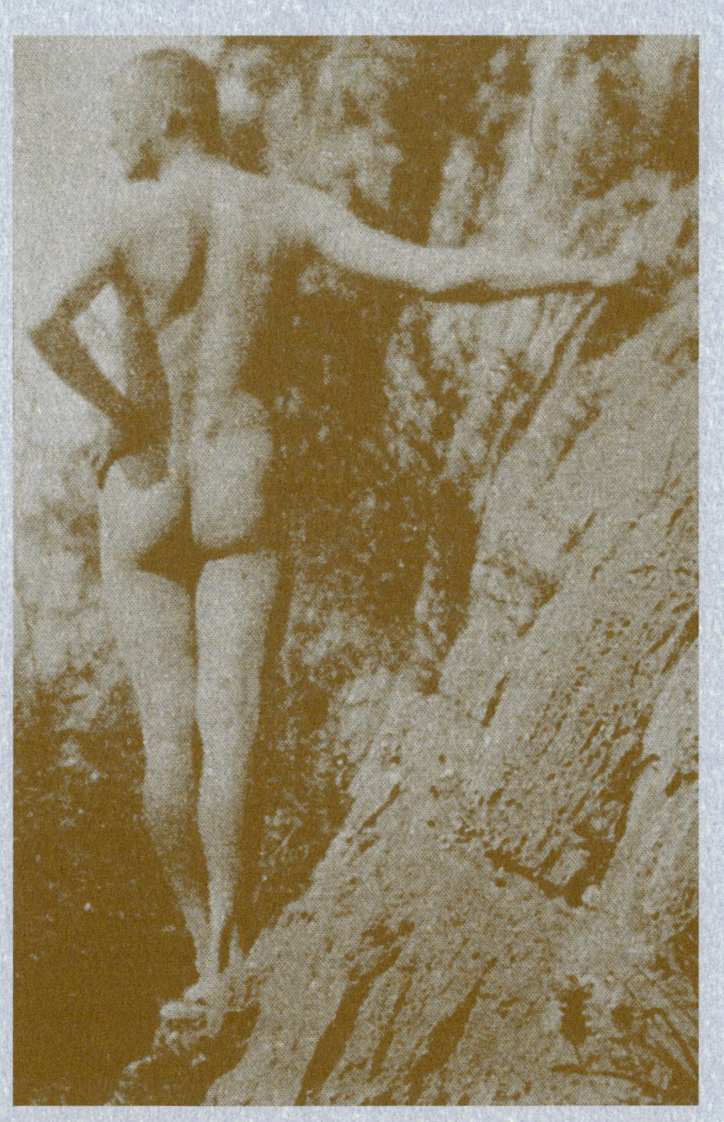

IX.5

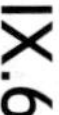 Below Is Serenity, above Is the Emptiness

IX.6

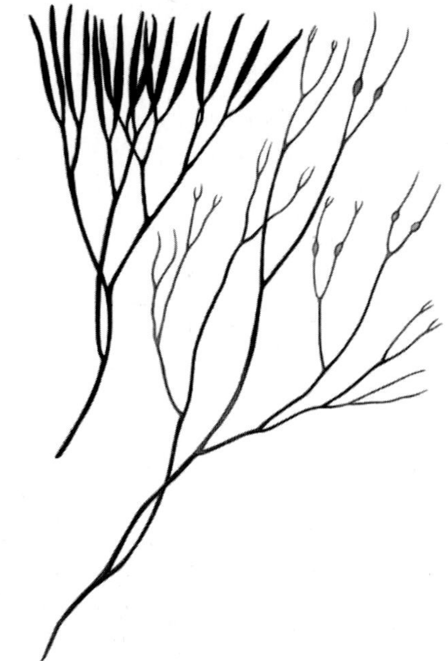

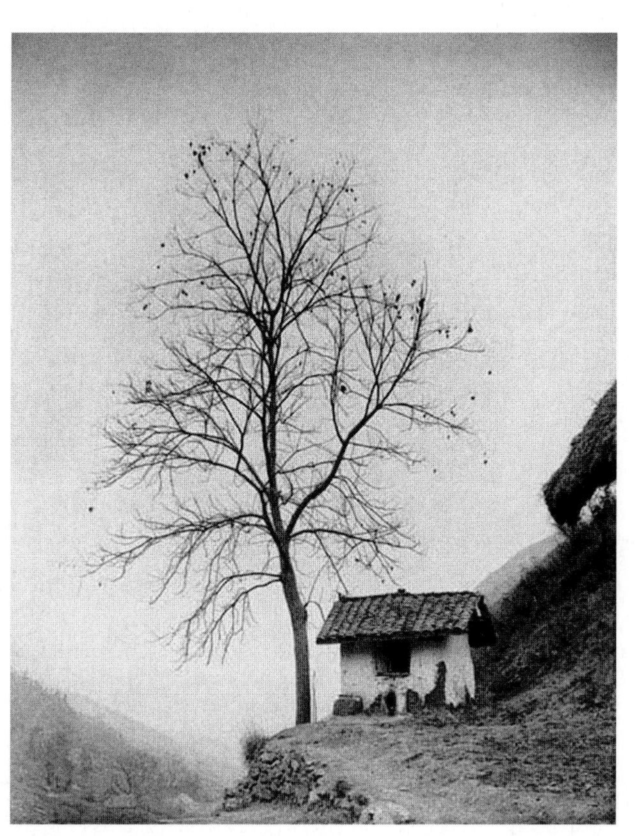

IX.7

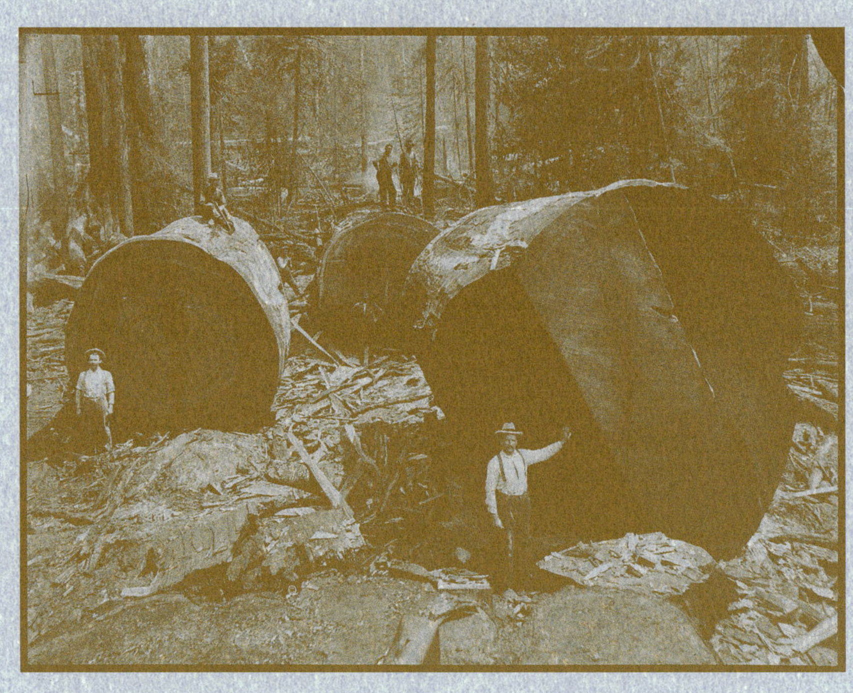

IX.8

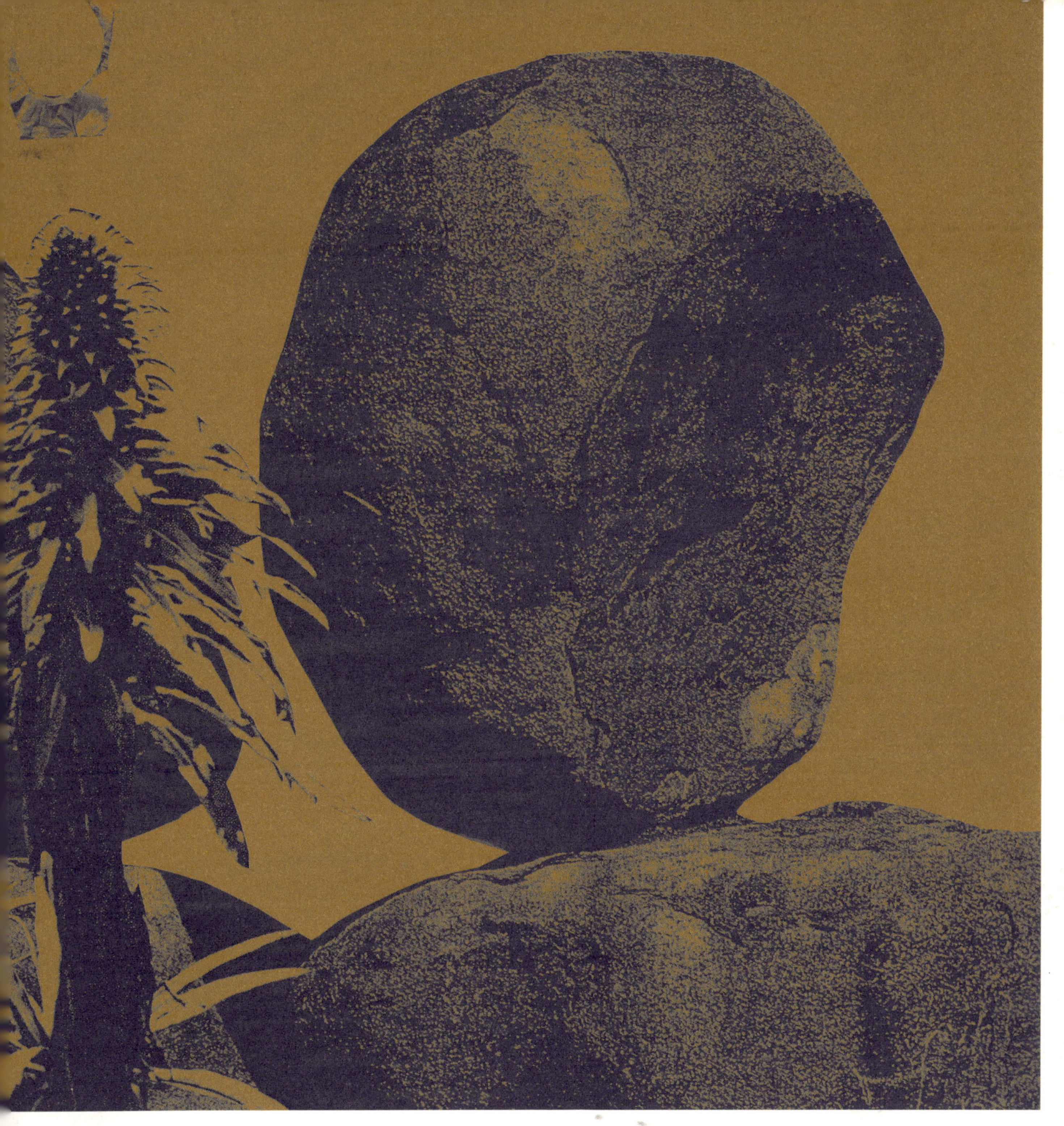

KIRSTINE ROEPSTORFF
HORIZONS OF THE MOVING MIND

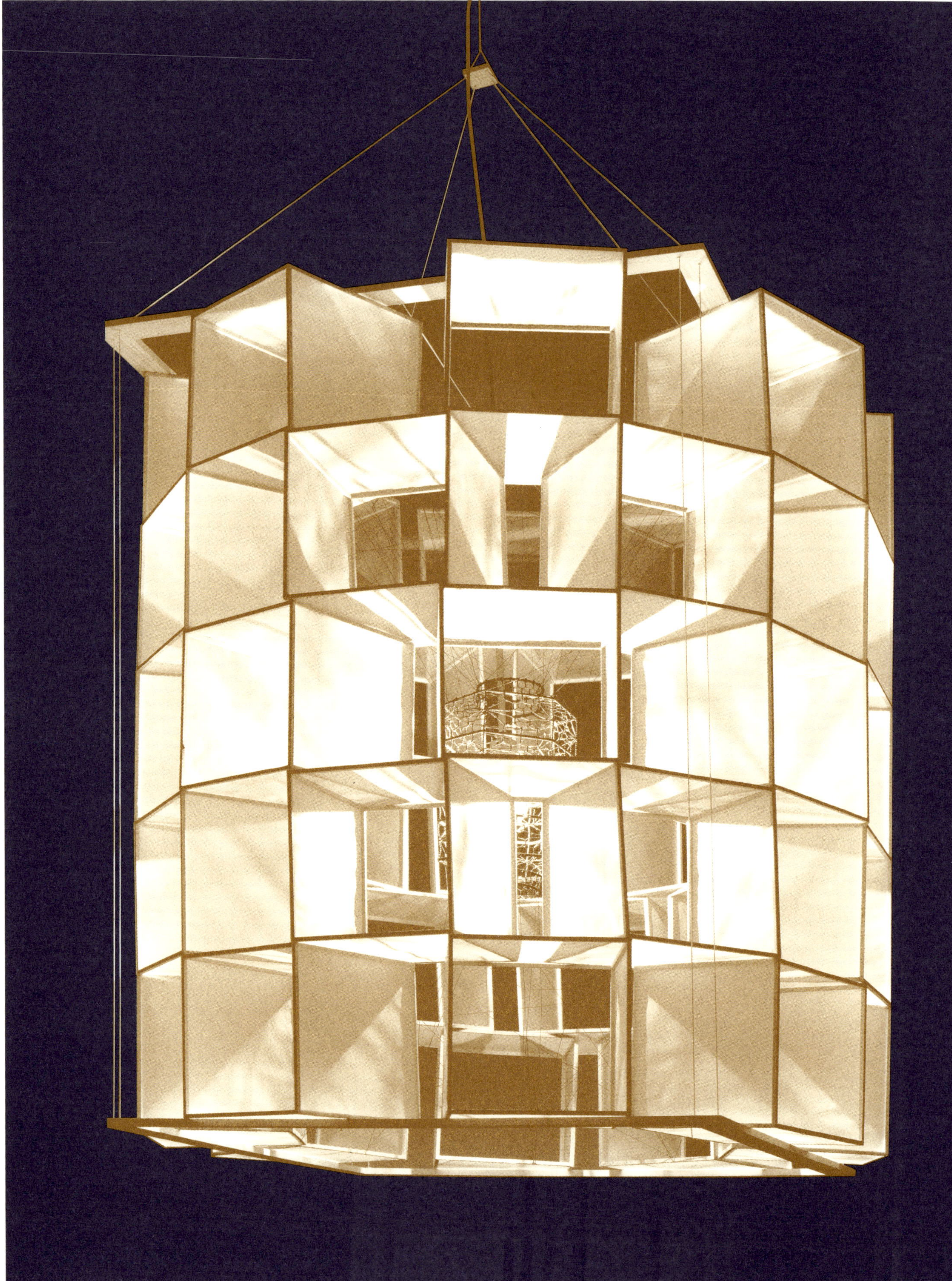